WeightWatchers®

COOK SMART nice 'n' spicy

Easy curries, spicy suppers and light meals
all with *ProPoints®* values

SIMON &
SCHUSTER
ILLUSTRATED

London · New York · Sydney · Toronto

A CBS COMPANY

First published in Great Britain by Simon & Schuster UK Ltd, 2011
A CBS Company

Copyright © 2011, Weight Watchers International, Inc.
Simon & Schuster Illustrated Books, Simon & Schuster UK Ltd, First Floor, 222 Gray's Inn Road, London WC1X 8HB

Weight Watchers Publications: Jane Griffiths, Imogen Prescott, Nina McKerlie, Cheryl Jackson and Selena Makepeace.

Recipes written by: Sue Ashworth, Sue Beveridge, Tamsin Burnett-Hall, Cas Clarke, Siân Davies, Roz Denny, Becky Johnson, Kim Morphew, Joy Skipper, Penny Stephens and Wendy Veale as well as Weight Watchers Leaders and Members.

Photography by: Iain Bagwell, Steve Baxter, Steve Lee and Juliet Piddington.
Design and typesetting by: Tiger Media Ltd.
Colour reproduction by Dot Gradations Ltd, UK
Printed and bound in China.

A CIP catalogue for this book is available from the British Library

ISBN 978-0-85720-689-3

1 3 5 7 9 10 8 6 4 2

Pictured on the front cover: Spicy Seafood Soup p12, Thai Beef Curry p90, Moroccan Lamb p144, Thai-style Chilli Beef p114.
Pictured on the Introduction: Potato Wedges with Chilli Dip p32, Tandoori Chicken p58, Vegetable Enchiladas p130, Red Pork Curry p116.

ProPoints® value logo: You'll find this easy to read **ProPoints** value logo on every recipe throughout this book. The logo represents the number of **ProPoints** values per serving each recipe contains. It is not an indication of the fillingness of a recipe.

Weight Watchers **ProPoints** Weight Loss System is a simple way to lose weight. As part of the Weight Watchers **ProPoints** plan you'll enjoy eating delicious, healthy, filling foods that help to keep you feeling satisfied for longer and in control of your portions.

V This symbol denotes a vegetarian recipe and assumes that, where relevant, free range eggs, vegetarian cheese, vegetarian virtually fat free fromage frais, vegetarian low fat crème fraîche and vegetarian low fat yogurts are used. Virtually fat free fromage frais, low fat crème fraîche and low fat yogurts may contain traces of gelatine so they are not always vegetarian. Please check the labels.

✱ This symbol denotes a dish that can be frozen. Unless otherwise stated, you can freeze the finished dish for up to 3 months. Defrost thoroughly and reheat until the dish is piping hot throughout.

Recipe notes
Egg size: Medium sized, unless otherwise stated.
Raw eggs: Only the freshest eggs should be used. Pregnant women, the elderly and children should avoid recipes with eggs that are not fully cooked or raw.
All fruits and vegetables: Medium sized, unless otherwise stated.
Stock: Stock cubes are used in recipes, unless otherwise stated. These should be prepared according to packet instructions.
Recipe timings: These are approximate and meant to be guidelines. Please note that the preparation time includes all the steps up to and following the main cooking time(s).
Microwaves: Timings and temperatures are for a standard 800 W microwave. If necessary, adjust your own microwave.
Low fat spread: Where a recipe states to use a low fat spread, a light spread with a fat content of no less than 38% should be used.
Low fat soft cheese: Where low fat soft cheese is specified in a recipe, this refers to soft cheese with a fat content of less than 5%.

Contents

Introduction

There's nothing like a little spice to add interest to your food, and *Cook Smart Nice 'n' Spicy* has plenty of fantastic ideas to help you jazz up your meals. From the freshness of chillies to the warmth of cumin and coriander, there are many ways to add spice without making your food too hot. However, if heat is your thing, just add a little more spice for a tongue-tingling sensation. It's simple and delicious.

About Weight Watchers

For more than 40 years Weight Watchers has been helping people around the world to lose weight using a long term sustainable approach. Weight Watchers successful weight loss system is based on four tried and trusted principles:

- Eating healthily
- Being more active
- Adjusting behaviour to help weight loss
- Getting support in weekly meetings

Our unique ***ProPoints*** system empowers you to manage your food plan and make wise recipe choices for a healthier, happier you.

Cooking with Spice

Spicy food does not just mean curries and there are so many different ways to add a little bit of spice to your food. Warm up a plain soup with a little cumin, jazz up an everyday salad with a dash of chilli, or liven up a stir fry with fresh Far Eastern flavours. Even a Sunday roast can be made more interesting with a coating of spice. Use the recipes in *Cook Smart Nice 'n' Spicy* to get you going and then start experimenting with your favourite dishes, adding fresh or ground spices to give them extra flavour.

By cooking your own meals you can control the amount of spice in your food as well as making sure it is lower in **ProPoints** values than takeaway alternatives.

Buying spices

It is always worth keeping a few spices in your store cupboard and it is always worth investing in some quality ingredients. This way you'll always have ingredients to create a tasty meal.

- Ground spices – check the dates on any dried spices in your cupboard and buy fresh ones if you need to. If you live near an ethnic grocer or supermarket, try buying from there instead of your regular supermarket. Prices can sometimes be lower and there will be a great choice. If possible, buy little and often so that the spices are as fresh as possible, and keep them in a cool dark place. Remember to replace them regularly if you don't use them up.

- Whole spices – if you want to grind your own spices you will need to invest in a pestle and mortar or a spice grinder, if you don't have one already. The colour and aroma of ready-ground spices can fade quickly and freshly ground ones have far more flavour.

- Curry and spice pastes – these are available in the ethnic foods departments of large supermarkets and from specialist retailers. Don't be afraid to use them and try a few to find the ones you like best.

- 'Ready prepared' lemongrass, ginger and garlic – these are great as an emergency standby, so don't be afraid to use them when necessary.

Adding more flavour

Toasting whole spices releases their aroma. If you are going to grind your own, you may want to toast them first by dry frying them in a pan for a minute or two until they give off a warm aroma. Be careful not to let them burn.

As well as adding spice, make the most of seasonal ingredients. From vibrant winter cabbages to spring asparagus and from juicy summer fruit to autumnal squashes, seasonal fresh fruit and vegetables taste far better than frozen or canned. And by ringing the changes you'll be eating a greater variety of fruit and vegetables throughout the year. You'll be less likely to get bored with the same old meals and may even find new favourite ingredients.

Even changing staple foods like pasta and rice can increase flavour. Try imported dried pastas, which have a wheaty, bread-like taste and will stay al dente better than most other brands. Or swap plain white rice for basmati or jasmine rice and see the difference. Try some different varieties to find the one you like the most.

Storing and Freezing

Once you have mastered the art of cooking delicious, healthy meals, you may want to make extra and store or freeze it for a later date. Store any leftovers in sealed containers in the fridge and use them up within a day or two. Many recipes can be frozen, as can individual ingredients, but it is important to make sure you know how to freeze safely.

- Wrap any food to be frozen in rigid containers or strong freezer bags. This is important to stop foods contaminating each other or getting freezer burn.

- Label the containers or bags with the contents and date – your freezer should have a star marking that tells you how long you can keep different types of frozen food.

- Never freeze warm food – always let it cool completely first.

- Never freeze food that has already been frozen and defrosted.

- Freeze food in portions, then you can take out as little or as much as you need each time.

- Defrost what you need in the fridge, making sure you put anything that might have juices, such as meat, on a covered plate or in a container.

Fresh food, such as raw meat or fish, should be wrapped and frozen as soon as possible. Most fruit and vegetables can be frozen by open freezing. Lay them out on a tray and freeze until solid, then pack them into bags. Some vegetables, such as peas, broccoli and broad beans can be blanched first by cooking for 2 minutes in boiling water. Drain and refresh under cold water then freeze once cold. Fresh herbs are great frozen – either seal leaves in bags or, for soft herbs such as basil and parsley, chop finely and add to ice cube trays with water. These are great for dropping into casseroles or soups straight from the freezer.

Some things cannot be frozen. Whole eggs do not freeze well, but yolks and eggs can be frozen separately. Vegetables with a high water content, such as salad leaves, celery and cucumber, will not freeze. Fried foods will be soggy if frozen, and sauces such as mayonnaise will separate when thawed and should not be frozen.

Starters,
Sides and Light Bites

Try a starter or light bite such as Vegetable Samosas, Spicy Beef Noodle Soup or Indian Pork. Or add a delicious side dish such as Easy Naan.

Be different and add interest
to a meal with a little spice

Spiced Parsnip Soup with Parsnip Crisps

Thick and warming, with home made crisps on the side.

Serves 4

500 g (1 lb 2 oz) parsnips
calorie controlled cooking spray
1 teaspoon ground cumin
1 teaspoon garam masala
1 litre (1¾ pints) vegetable stock
salt and freshly ground black pepper

3 ProPoints values per serving
10 ProPoints values per recipe

92 calories per serving

Takes **30 minutes**

V

* recommended (soup only)

1 Preheat the oven to Gas Mark 6/200°C/fan oven 180°C. Peel all the parsnips, leaving one whole and cutting the rest into chunks.

2 Lightly spray a large, lidded, non stick saucepan with the cooking spray and heat until hot. Add the chopped parsnips and spices and stir fry for 1 minute. Add the stock, bring to the boil, cover and simmer for 10 minutes or until the parsnips are tender.

3 Meanwhile, using a vegetable peeler, cut the remaining parsnip into ribbons. Spread out on a non stick baking tray and lightly spray with the cooking spray. Sprinkle over a little seasoning and bake for 5–10 minutes until golden and crisp.

4 Remove the soup from the heat and transfer to a liquidiser, or use a hand held blender, and whizz until smooth. Return to the pan and warm through.

5 Serve the soup hot with the parsnip crisps on the side.

Tips If you prefer a spicier soup, add ½ teaspoon of chilli powder with the other spices.

You can make the soup in advance, but the crisps are best when fresh.

Spicy Seafood Soup

Serve this with a 25 g (1 oz) slice of garlic bread per person, or a 30 g (1¼ oz) slice of fresh crusty bread per person, both for 3 *ProPoints* values per serving.

Serves 4

calorie controlled cooking spray
1 onion, sliced
1 leek, sliced
1 garlic clove, chopped finely
400 g can chopped tomatoes
300 ml (10 fl oz) white wine
425 ml (15 fl oz) hot fish or vegetable stock
1 bouquet garni
1 tablespoon chopped fresh parsley, plus extra
  to garnish
½ teaspoon dried dill (optional)
1 bay leaf
¼ teaspoon cayenne pepper
¼ teaspoon paprika
350 g (12 oz) frozen seafood cocktail
75 g (2¾ oz) haddock fillet, cubed
100 g (3½ oz) mussels in shells, scrubbed
salt and freshly ground black pepper

5 *ProPoints* values per serving
18 *ProPoints* values per recipe

199 calories per serving

Takes **15 minutes** to prepare
25 minutes to cook

not recommended

1 Heat a large non stick saucepan and spray with the cooking spray. Add the onion, leek and garlic and cook over a medium heat, stirring often, until the vegetables look transparent, but not browned, about 5–8 minutes.

2 Add the tomatoes, white wine and stock. Stir in all the herbs and spices. Tip in all the seafood, making sure that you discard any mussels that are damaged or open. Heat until just simmering, then reduce the heat to low and simmer gently for 10–15 minutes.

3 Discard any mussels that have failed to open and remove the bay leaf and bouquet garni. Check the seasoning, adding more to taste if needed. Ladle into warmed soup bowls and serve at once, garnished with the extra chopped parsley.

Tips Keep packs of frozen mixed seafood in your freezer, at the ready to make this delicious recipe.

Serve as a light meal for two instead, for just 9 *ProPoints* values per serving.

Spicy Beef Noodle Soup

Serves 4

225 g (8 oz) sirloin steak, sliced thinly
250 g (9 oz) dried egg noodles
200 g (7 oz) sugarsnap peas, mange tout or green beans, sliced lengthways
25 g (1 oz) fresh coriander, chopped (optional)

For the marinade

1 tablespoon soy sauce
1 garlic clove, chopped finely
2.5 cm (1 inch) fresh root ginger, chopped finely
1 tablespoon honey
1 small red chilli, de-seeded and chopped finely, or ½ teaspoon dried chilli flakes

For the soup

2 litres (3½ pints) beef or chicken stock
1 garlic clove, crushed
1 lemongrass stick, chopped roughly, or 1 tablespoon dried lemongrass
1 small red chilli, de-seeded and chopped, or ½ teaspoon dried chilli flakes
1 star anise
1 cm (½ inch) fresh root ginger, chopped, or 1 teaspoon ground ginger

10 *ProPoints* values per serving
39 *ProPoints* values per recipe

377 calories per serving

Takes **10 minutes** to prepare + **30 minutes** marinating **20 minutes** to cook

✳ not recommended

1 Mix the marinade ingredients together in a shallow bowl and add the steak strips. Toss to coat and leave to marinate for up to 30 minutes.

2 Meanwhile, place the soup ingredients in a large saucepan and bring to the boil. Turn the heat down to a simmer.

3 Bring a second saucepan of water to the boil, add the noodles and cook according to the packet instructions. Drain thoroughly.

4 Heat a frying pan until very hot, and brown the marinated steak strips for 1 minute on each side, then transfer to a plate to rest.

5 Strain the soup, return to the pan and bring back to the boil. Add the sugarsnap peas, mange tout or green beans and cook for 2 minutes.

6 Divide the noodles between four serving bowls and add the beef.

7 Pour the soup over the noodles and steak. Serve sprinkled with the coriander, if using.

Courgette Pancakes with Spicy Relish

Delicious little courgette cakes to dip into a fiery and spicy relish.

Serves 1

2 tablespoons plain flour
2 tablespoons skimmed milk
2 courgettes, grated coarsely
1 egg white
calorie controlled cooking spray
salt and freshly ground black pepper

For the spicy relish

150 g (5½ oz) cherry tomatoes, quartered
½ red onion, chopped finely
1 small red chilli, de-seeded and chopped finely
juice of a lemon
a dash of Tabasco sauce
a dash of Worcestershire sauce
a small bunch of fresh coriander, basil, parsley or mint, chopped finely

5 _ProPoints_ values per serving
5 _ProPoints_ values per recipe

280 calories per serving

Takes **20 minutes**

(without the Worcestershire sauce)

not recommended

1 Put the flour and seasoning into a bowl and stir in the milk. Add the courgettes and mix together, then set aside.

2 Make the relish by mixing all the ingredients together in a bowl.

3 In a clean, grease-free bowl, whisk the egg white until stiff, then gently fold it into the courgette mixture with a large metal spoon.

4 Heat a large non stick frying pan and spray with the cooking spray. Drop 4 tablespoonfuls of the courgette mixture into the pan (this will use up all the mixture).

5 Cook the pancakes for 3–4 minutes, then flip them over with a palette knife and cook the other side for 3–4 minutes, until golden brown. Put the pancakes on a plate and serve with the relish.

Spicy Sausage and Bean Salad

A really colourful salad full of robust flavours.

Serves 4

8 x 20 g (¾ oz) thin low fat sausages
1 small red onion, chopped finely
1 small red chilli, de-seeded and chopped finely
(or 1 teaspoon dried chilli flakes)
4 ripe tomatoes, sliced
2 x 400 g cans cannellini beans, drained and
rinsed
a small bunch of fresh parsley, basil or
coriander, chopped
salt and freshly ground black pepper

For the dressing

2 tablespoons balsamic vinegar
4 teaspoons olive oil
1 teaspoon Tabasco sauce
1 tablespoon Worcestershire sauce

7 ProPoints values per serving
27 ProPoints values per recipe

275 calories per serving

Takes **20 minutes** + **30 minutes**
marinating (optional)

✳ not recommended

1 Preheat the grill to medium heat and grill the sausages for about
5 minutes on each side until browned and cooked through. Set aside
to cool.

2 Meanwhile, place all the dressing ingredients in a clean screw top jar
and shake until mixed. Place the onion, chilli, tomatoes, beans and
herbs in a bowl and season. Pour over the dressing.

3 Chop the sausages into small pieces, add to the salad and toss
everything together. Leave to marinate for as long as possible before
serving.

Variations Try a tablespoon of wholegrain mustard in the dressing
instead of the Tabasco and Worcestershire sauce, and you could omit
the chilli too. The **ProPoints** values will remain the same.

You could also use flageolet beans instead of the cannellini beans for
the same **ProPoints** values per serving.

Spicy Duck Salad

This delicious salad is infused with a blend of seven classic Thai spices, including chilli, cumin, coriander, cinnamon and cloves. Serve in a warmed medium (42 g/1½ oz) soft flour tortilla per person, for an additional 3 **ProPoints** values per serving.

Serves 2

2 teaspoons Thai 7 spice
2 x 150 g (5½ oz) skinless boneless duck breasts
calorie controlled cooking spray
3 spring onions, sliced finely
50 g (1¾ oz) mild or hot piquante peppers (e.g. Peppadew), drained and sliced finely
½ papaya, peeled, de-seeded and diced
2 celery sticks, sliced finely
2 tablespoons reduced fat mayonnaise
½ small Iceberg lettuce, shredded finely

7 **ProPoints** values per serving
13 **ProPoints** values per recipe

325 **calories** per serving

Takes **21 minutes**

✳ not recommended

1 Rub the Thai spices all over the duck breasts. Heat a non stick frying pan until hot and spray the duck with the cooking spray. Cook the duck breasts on a medium-low heat for 10 minutes, turning halfway. Remove the duck from the pan and wrap in foil. Set aside for 5 minutes.

2 Meanwhile, mix together the spring onions, peppers, papaya, celery and mayonnaise. Divide the lettuce between two plates and top each with some of the papaya salad. Slice the duck breasts on the diagonal and serve on top of the salad.

Indian Pork

A fast dish for two that could be served for lunch or as a light supper.

Serves 2

200 g (7 oz) lean pork tenderloin, cut into 5 mm (¼ inch) slices
½ teaspoon garam masala
a generous pinch of hot chilli powder
½ teaspoon caraway seeds, crushed
75 g (2¾ oz) very ripe mango, peeled and chopped
75 g (2¾ oz) 0% fat Greek yogurt
60 g (2 oz) baby spinach leaves, rinsed
2 large tomatoes, chopped roughly
calorie controlled cooking spray
salt and freshly ground black pepper

4 ProPoints values per serving
7 ProPoints values per recipe

204 calories per serving

Takes **20 minutes**

not recommended

1 Take a slice of pork and place it between two sheets of cling film. Using the end of a rolling pin, hammer the meat until it is paper thin. Repeat with the remaining slices and transfer to a bowl.

2 Add the garam masala, chilli powder and caraway seeds. Toss to coat the pork in the spices. Set aside.

3 Put the mango and yogurt into a food processor, or use a hand held blender, and whizz until smooth. Season and set aside. Divide the spinach between two plates and scatter over the tomatoes.

4 Heat a griddle pan or non stick frying pan until really hot. Spray the pork slices with the cooking spray, then cook the pork slices for 3–4 minutes, turning until cooked and slightly charred. Divide between the plates, drizzle with the mango dressing and serve.

Tip If fresh mango isn't available, use canned mango slices in natural juice, drained. The **ProPoints** values will remain the same.

Sweet and Spicy Crab Cakes

This dish would be lovely served al fresco with a large zero *ProPoints* value green salad.

Serves 4

700 g (1 lb 9 oz) sweet potatoes, peeled and cut into chunks
2 garlic cloves, peeled
2 x 170 g cans white crabmeat in brine or water, drained
1 red chilli, de-seeded and diced
3 tablespoons chopped fresh coriander
finely grated zest of 2 limes
calorie controlled cooking spray
freshly ground black pepper

For the salsa

4 vine tomatoes, de-seeded and diced
10 cm (4 inches) cucumber, de-seeded and diced
4 spring onions, sliced
juice of 2 limes, plus extra lime wedges, to serve

6 *ProPoints* values per serving
24 *ProPoints* values per recipe

236 calories per serving

Takes **15 minutes** to prepare + chilling,
10–15 minutes to cook

recommended (crab cakes only)

1 Bring a large lidded pan of water to the boil, add the sweet potatoes and garlic, cover and simmer for 10–15 minutes until tender. Drain thoroughly, return to the pan and place over a low heat for 30 seconds to allow any excess water to evaporate. Mash, squashing the garlic in with the potatoes, and leave until cool enough to handle.

2 Stir the crabmeat into the mash with the chilli, coriander and lime zest. Season with black pepper. Shape the mixture into four cakes and place on a plate in the fridge for 30 minutes.

3 Meanwhile, to make the salsa, combine all the ingredients (except the lime wedges), cover and chill.

4 Spray a non stick frying pan with the cooking spray and heat until hot. Cook the cakes for 3–5 minutes until golden and hot, turning once. Serve with the salsa and lime wedges.

Curry-style Mushrooms on Toast

A quick and simple snack that tastes delicious.

Serves 1

1 medium slice wholemeal bread
50 g (1¾ oz) mushrooms, halved or quartered, depending on size
2 tablespoons skimmed milk
30 g (1¼ oz) aubergine pickle

6 _ProPoints_ values per serving
6 _ProPoints_ values per recipe

203 calories per serving

Takes **5 minutes**

V

* not recommended

1 Toast the bread.

2 Meanwhile, heat the remaining ingredients in a small pan until the mushrooms have softened slightly.

3 Serve the mushrooms and sauce on the toasted bread.

Rocket, Prawn and Mango Salad

An appetising and colourful salad that looks great as part of a buffet at parties. It's also low in *ProPoints* values and very easy to prepare.

Serves 6

500 g (1 lb 2 oz) cooked and peeled tiger prawns
1 large ripe mango, peeled and sliced
¾ cucumber, cut into half moon slices
80 g (3 oz) wild rocket
6 tablespoons sweet chilli sauce
juice of 1½ limes
3 tablespoons chopped fresh coriander

2 *ProPoints* values per serving
15 *ProPoints* values per recipe

139 calories per serving

Takes **15 minutes**

not recommended

1 Toss the tiger prawns together with the mango and cucumber slices. Heap the prawn mixture on to a large serving plate and scatter the rocket on top.

2 Whisk the chilli sauce with the lime juice and coriander and drizzle over the salad just before serving.

Vegetable Samosas

These samosas are very low in *ProPoints* values and are ideal for buffets and snacks.

Makes 24

2 carrots, peeled and diced
calorie controlled cooking spray
2 shallots or 1 small onion, chopped finely
1 garlic clove, chopped finely
150 g (5½ oz) spinach, fresh or frozen
100 g (3½ oz) potatoes, peeled and diced
1 tablespoon Indian balti or tandoori curry paste
100 g (3½ oz) frozen peas
juice of ½ a lime
8 x 45 g (1½ oz) filo pastry sheets measuring 28 x 43 cm (11 x 17 inches)
salt and freshly ground black pepper

For the raita

4 tablespoons low fat natural yogurt
½ small garlic clove, crushed
a small bunch of fresh mint, chopped finely, plus extra to garnish

1 *ProPoints* value per serving
34 *ProPoints* values per recipe

60 calories per serving

Takes **1 hour** to prepare, **15 minutes** to cook

V

* not recommended

1 Bring a pan of water to the boil, add the carrots and cook until tender. Drain and set aside. Spray a non stick baking tray with the cooking spray.

2 Meanwhile, heat a large non stick frying pan and spray with the cooking spray. Fry the shallots or onion and garlic until golden. Add the carrots, spinach, potatoes, curry paste, peas, lime juice and seasoning. Stir together and cook for 5 minutes. Preheat the oven to Gas Mark 7/220°C/fan oven 200°C.

3 Lay one sheet of filo pastry on a clean dry work surface and cut lengthways into three equal strips. Spray with the cooking spray and place 2 teaspoons of the vegetable mixture about 1 cm (½ inch) from one end of a strip. Pick up the corner of the pastry strip and fold over the vegetable mixture to create a triangular shaped parcel with two open seams. Flip the whole parcel over, wrapping along the length of the filo pastry strip and keeping the triangular shape. Continue until all the pastry is used up and then spray the samosa with the cooking spray. Lay it on the prepared baking tray and repeat with the remaining filo pastry strips.

4 Bake for 15 minutes, until the pastry is golden and crisp. Leave to cool slightly.

5 Meanwhile, make the raita by stirring together all the ingredients with a little seasoning. Spoon into a bowl to serve and garnish with the mint sprigs.

Tip If using frozen pastry, allow it to thaw in the pack and then take out the sheets and stack them on a cloth. While you work, cover the sheets with a slightly damp cloth and use the sheets one at a time. This will help to keep the filo pastry moist as it dries out very quickly.

Hot Turkey Salad

If you're faced with an abundance of leftover turkey, why not transform it into a delicious turkey salad, served with a lively chilli dressing to give it a bit of a kick?

Serves 4

1 head Chinese leaf, shredded
3 celery sticks, finely sliced
1 red or yellow pepper, de-seeded and cut into fine strips
6 spring onions or 1 small red onion, finely sliced
2 tablespoons stir fry oil or sesame oil
1–2 teaspoons chilli sauce
1 tablespoon lemon juice
1 tablespoon soy sauce
350 g (12 oz) cooked turkey, shredded
freshly ground black pepper
snipped chives or cress, to garnish

5 ProPoints values per serving
21 ProPoints values per recipe

231 calories per serving

Takes **20 minutes**

✱ not recommended

1 Mix together the Chinese leaf, celery, pepper and spring onions or onion. Divide between four serving bowls or plates.

2 Make the dressing by mixing together 1 tablespoon of stir fry oil or sesame oil with the chilli sauce, lemon juice and soy sauce. Season with black pepper; you won't need any salt because the soy sauce is salty.

3 Heat the remaining oil in a non stick wok or frying pan. Add the strips of cooked turkey, stir frying them over a high heat until crispy and brown. Pile on top of the salads.

4 Sprinkle the salads with the dressing, then serve, garnished with snipped chives or cress.

Tip Stir fry oil is flavoured with ginger and garlic and makes a tasty base for the spicy salad dressing, so don't just think of it for stir frying.

Variation Instead of Chinese leaf, use a Little Gem lettuce and a head of chicory, or a bag of mixed salad leaves. The **ProPoints** values will remain the same.

Chilli Tuna Filling

Spoon this zingy tuna filling on to a 225 g (8 oz) jacket potato, baked in its skin, with crunchy salad leaves, for an additional 5 *ProPoints* values.

Serves 1

80 g can tuna in brine, drained
1 tablespoon low fat natural yogurt
1 tablespoon low fat mayonnaise
1 tablespoon sweet chilli sauce
1 tablespoon chopped fresh coriander
½ tablespoon lime juice
salt and freshly ground black pepper

4 *ProPoints* values per serving
4 *ProPoints* values per recipe

160 calories per serving

Takes **5 minutes**

not recommended

1 Flake the tuna into a bowl, add the remaining ingredients and mix well. Season to taste.

Chargrilled Aubergine and Lamb Salad

Tahini is a smooth ground sesame seed paste and when combined with yogurt it makes a fantastic dressing.

Serves 1

15 g (½ oz) pine nut kernels
100 g (3½ oz) aubergine, sliced thinly
¼ teaspoon smoked paprika
calorie controlled cooking spray
½ tablespoon tahini
1 tablespoon 0% fat Greek yogurt
juice of ½ a lemon
1 teaspoon clear honey
½ teaspoon garam masala
30 g (1¼ oz) slice roast lamb, shredded
1 tablespoon mustard cress

8 ProPoints values per serving
8 ProPoints values per recipe

327 calories per serving

Takes **18 minutes**

not recommended

1 To toast the pine nut kernels, heat a dry non stick frying pan until hot. Sprinkle over the pine nuts and gently cook for 1 minute, shaking the pan until golden. Transfer to a bowl immediately and leave to go cold.

2 Sprinkle the aubergine slices with the paprika and spray with the cooking spray. Heat a griddle or non stick frying pan until hot and cook the aubergine slices for 5–8 minutes, turning until chargrilled and cooked. Transfer to a plate.

3 In a small bowl, mix together the tahini, yogurt, lemon juice, honey and garam masala until smooth. Top the aubergine slices with the lamb and scatter over the cress and pine nut kernels. Spoon over the dressing and sprinkle with a little paprika. Serve immediately.

Potato Wedges with Chilli Dip

The crispy crust on these potatoes will give you all the satisfaction of a plate of chips without the fat.

Serves 2

300 g (10½ oz) baking potatoes, cut into wedges
2 teaspoons dried oregano or herbes de Provence
2 garlic cloves, crushed
salt and freshly ground black pepper

For the chilli dip

calorie controlled cooking spray
a bunch of spring onions, chopped finely
1 garlic clove, crushed
200 g can chopped tomatoes
1 red chilli, de-seeded and chopped finely
1 tablespoon balsamic vinegar
a small bunch of fresh basil or coriander, chopped

3 ProPoints values per serving
7 ProPoints values per recipe

164 calories per serving

Takes **15 minutes** to prepare,
35 minutes to cook

V

* recommended (chilli dip only)

1 Bring a pan of water to the boil, add the potatoes and simmer for 10–15 minutes, until just tender. Preheat the oven to Gas Mark 6/ 200°C/fan oven 180°C.

2 For the chilli dip, heat a medium non stick saucepan and spray with the cooking spray. Stir fry the spring onions and garlic for a few minutes, until softened, and then add the other ingredients. Bring to the boil and simmer gently for 10 minutes until reduced and thickened. Season and pour into a serving bowl.

3 Meanwhile, drain the potatoes and place them in a roasting tin. Spray with the cooking spray, season and scatter with the herbs and garlic. Toss together, then roast for 20 minutes, turning occasionally, until golden and crisp and cooked through. Serve hot with the chilli dip.

Curried Chicken Dippers

These are ideal for a light bite or for a buffet.

For the dippers

100 g (3½ oz) low fat natural yogurt
1 tablespoon medium curry powder
2 garlic cloves, crushed
½ teaspoon ground turmeric
2 tablespoons lemon juice
2 tablespoons chopped fresh coriander
½ teaspoon salt
350 g (12 oz) skinless boneless chicken breasts, cut into long thin strips

For the dip

150g (5½ oz) low fat natural yogurt
1 tablespoon mint jelly
100 g (3½ oz) cucumber, diced finely

4 ProPoints values per serving
15 ProPoints values per recipe

156 calories per serving

Takes **20 minutes** + chilling
+ **20 minutes** marinating

recommended (dippers only)

1 Mix together the yogurt, curry powder, garlic, turmeric, lemon juice, coriander and salt. Spoon this mixture over the chicken and stir to coat all the strips well. Cover and leave to marinate for 20 minutes. Preheat the grill to medium and line the grill pan with foil.

2 Meanwhile, prepare the dip. Beat together the yogurt, mint jelly and cucumber and chill in the fridge until required.

3 Place the chicken strips under the grill and cook for 10 minutes, turning frequently, until they are cooked through.

4 Serve the dippers hot or cold with the dip alongside.

Roasted Aubergine Dip

Try this dip for a change – it's so easy to make, tastes wonderful and has no *ProPoints* values.

Serves 2

1 large aubergine, cut in half lengthways
1 teaspoon soy sauce
1 teaspoon sweet chilli sauce
½ teaspoon lemon juice
1 tablespoon chopped fresh coriander
2 spring onions, sliced finely
zero *ProPoints* value crudités, e.g. carrots and
celery, to serve

0 *ProPoints* values per serving
0 *ProPoints* values per recipe

35 calories per serving

Takes **8 minutes** to prepare,
30 minutes to cook + cooling

V

✱ not recommended

1 Preheat the oven to Gas Mark 6/200°C/fan oven 180°C. Score the aubergine flesh with a sharp knife. Place on a non stick baking tray and cook for 30 minutes.

2 Remove from the oven, leave to cool and then scrape away the skin from the aubergine flesh. Discard the skin. Place the flesh in a food processor with the soy sauce, chilli sauce and lemon juice. Whizz until smooth.

3 Mix in the coriander and spring onions and serve with the zero *ProPoints* value crudités.

Thai Cucumber Salad

This is a very easy salad to make and only 1 *ProPoints* value per serving.

Serves 2

18 cm (7 inch) cucumber, halved, de-seeded and sliced thinly
2 spring onions, sliced
½ red chilli, de-seeded and sliced thinly

For the dressing
1 tablespoon lime juice
2 tablespoons soy sauce
1 tablespoon water
2 teaspoons sugar

1 *ProPoints* value per serving
2 *ProPoints* values per recipe

34 calories per serving

Takes **5 minutes** to prepare

not recommended

1 Mix together the dressing ingredients.

2 In a large bowl, combine the salad ingredients and pour over the dressing.

3 Divide the salad between two shallow bowls and serve.

Tip Add 1 tablespoon of fish sauce when making the dressing for a more authentic Thai flavour. Thai fish sauce is now widely available in supermarkets. The *ProPoints* values will remain the same.

Curried Tuna Pasta Salad

Quick and easy to prepare, this is a great pasta salad to take to work.

Serves 1

**50 g (1¾ oz) dried mini pasta shapes,
  e.g. conchigliette**
80 g can tuna in spring water or brine, drained

For the dressing
½ teaspoon medium curry powder
60 g (2 oz) low fat natural yogurt
½ red or yellow pepper, de-seeded and diced
75 g (2¾ oz) cucumber, diced
salt and freshly ground black pepper

7 ProPoints values per serving
7 ProPoints values per recipe

285 calories per serving

Takes **7 minutes**

not recommended

1 Bring a pan of water to the boil, add the pasta and cook according to the packet instructions until tender.

2 Meanwhile, to make the dressing, mix the curry powder and seasoning into the yogurt, then stir in the diced pepper and cucumber.

3 Drain the pasta and rinse in cold water. Shake dry then stir into the dressing. Flake in the tuna, mix together and serve.

Aloo Gobi

Spice up your vegetables with this easy but tasty dish. 'Aloo' means potato and 'gobi' means cauliflower.

Serves 4

calorie controlled cooking spray
3 onions, chopped
1 cauliflower, cut into florets
300 g (10½ oz) potatoes, peeled and chopped
2 teaspoons grated fresh root ginger
2 tomatoes, chopped
¼ teaspoon cayenne pepper
½ teaspoon turmeric
1½ teaspoons ground coriander
½ teaspoon garam masala
½ teaspoon cumin seeds
1½ teaspoons salt

2 *ProPoints* values per serving
7 *ProPoints* values per recipe

126 calories per serving

Takes **10 minutes** to prepare,
30 minutes to cook

V

* not recommended

1 Heat a large, lidded, non stick saucepan, spray with the cooking spray and sauté the onions for 3–4 minutes until beginning to soften.

2 Add the cauliflower florets, potatoes, ginger, tomatoes, cayenne pepper, turmeric, ground coriander and salt and mix really well to coat the vegetables in the spices.

3 Pour in 100 ml (3½ fl oz) of water, bring to a simmer and then cover and simmer gently for 15 minutes.

4 Add the garam masala and cumin seeds, mix well and then cover again and cook for a further 15 minutes until the potatoes are tender. Serve hot.

Tip The heat in this recipe comes from the cayenne pepper, so just adjust the amount you use according to how hot you like your food.

Variation For an even more substantial dish, add a drained 410 g can of chick peas in step 4 with the garam masala and cumin seeds. The *ProPoints* values will then be 4 per serving.

Tarka Dahl

'Tarka' is a spiced butter or oil that is added to a dish just before serving. 'Dahl' is a generic word for lentils, of which many types are used in Indian cuisine.

1 Place the lentils in a large lidded saucepan with the onion, ginger and vegetable stock. Bring to the boil and simmer, covered, for 15 minutes until the lentils have absorbed most of the liquid and broken down to a mushy pulp.

2 Heat the oil, garlic, mustard seeds and cumin seeds together in a small non stick pan for 1 minute or until golden (don't let the garlic burn). Stir in the tomato purée and cook for 30 seconds. Add a ladleful of lentils to the pan, stir everything together, then return everything to the lentil pan. Stir in the lemon juice and add seasoning to taste.

3 Serve garnished with the diced tomatoes and chopped coriander.

Tips You can turn this into a hearty warming soup, simply by doubling the amount of stock used. The **ProPoints** values will remain the same.

If you enjoy cooking Indian food, it really is worth keeping a stock of some whole spices such as cumin seeds and black mustard seeds, as they have a more intense flavour than ready ground spices.

Spicy Chick Pea Patties

These delicious little patties are similar to falafel. Serve with a large mixed salad of lettuce, cucumber, cherry tomatoes and red pepper, for no additional *ProPoints* values.

Serves 4

2 teaspoons cumin seeds
2 teaspoons coriander seeds
2 x 400 g cans chick peas, drained and rinsed
4 spring onions, chopped
1 tablespoon chopped fresh red chilli
2 egg whites
calorie controlled cooking spray

4 *ProPoints* values per serving
18 *ProPoints* values per recipe

160 calories per serving

Takes **10 minutes**

V

* not recommended

1 Lightly crush the cumin and coriander seeds in a pestle and mortar (see Tip). Place the chick peas in a food processor, or use a hand held blender, and roughly blend. Add the seeds, spring onions, chilli and egg whites and pulse a couple of times until blended. Divide the mixture into eight and shape into patties.

2 Spray a non stick frying pan with the cooking spray and heat until hot. Add the patties and cook for 4–5 minutes, turning occasionally until golden. Take care when turning them as they are quite fragile. Serve two warm patties each.

Tip If you don't have a pestle and mortar, use the end of a rolling pin to crush the seeds in a small bowl.

Easy Naan

There is nothing nicer than home made bread to serve alongside your favourite curry and, better still, these are faster and certainly tastier than a takeaway.

Serves 6

calorie controlled cooking spray
125 ml (4 fl oz) semi skimmed milk
1 egg, beaten
2 teaspoons caster sugar
1 tablespoon low fat natural yogurt
300 g (10½ oz) plain flour, plus 2 tablespoons
  extra for kneading
a pinch of salt
½ teaspoon bicarbonate of soda
1 teaspoon black onion seeds
3 garlic cloves, crushed
½ x 25 g packet fresh coriander, chopped finely
1 tablespoon low fat spread, melted

7 ProPoints values per serving
42 ProPoints values per recipe

249 calories per serving

Takes **24 minutes**

V

✱ recommended

1 Preheat the oven to Gas Mark 7/220°C/fan oven 200°C. Spray a baking tray with the cooking spray and put in the oven to heat.

2 In a jug, mix together the milk, egg, sugar and yogurt. Set aside. In a large bowl, mix together the flour, pinch of salt, bicarbonate of soda, onion seeds and garlic. Pour the milk mixture into the flour mixture and stir quickly to combine into a soft dough.

3 Turn the dough out on to a lightly floured surface and knead for 5 minutes. Divide the dough into six equal pieces. Press each piece of dough into the coriander and then roll out until 5 mm (¼ inch) thick.

4 Remove the baking tray from the oven, transfer the dough to the tray, brush with the melted low fat spread and bake for 8–10 minutes until risen and golden. Serve warm.

Curries and Chillies

Try making your own curries with all the flavour of your takeaway favourites but without the cream and oil. From Chicken Tikka Kebabs to Beef Rhogan Josh, Lamb Kofta Curry and Aubergine Madras, these are easy to prepare and full of flavour. Many of these dishes are great with 60 g (2 oz) of dried rice per person, cooked according to packet instructions, for an extra 6 *ProPoints* values per serving.

Replace the weekly takeaway with a delicious home made version

Creamy Beef Passanda

This is the perfect mild, creamy curry for winter evenings.

Serves 1

calorie controlled cooking spray
110 g (4 oz) lean rump steak
1 large shallot, chopped finely
½ teaspoon garlic purée
½ teaspoon ground coriander
a generous pinch of ground turmeric
¼ teaspoon ground cumin
¼ teaspoon mild curry powder
2 teaspoons ground almonds
2 tablespoons half fat crème fraîche
salt and freshly ground black pepper

---

11 ProPoints values per serving
11 ProPoints values per recipe

415 calories per serving

Takes **15 minutes**

not recommended

1 Heat a non stick frying pan and spray with the cooking spray. Cook the steak for 4–6 minutes, turning halfway, until cooked to your liking. Transfer to a plate and cover loosely with foil to keep warm. Set aside.

2 Spray the pan again with the cooking spray and gently cook the shallot for 3 minutes. Add the garlic purée, coriander, turmeric, cumin and curry powder. Cook for a further 30 seconds.

3 Add the almonds, crème fraîche and 3 tablespoons of cold water. Bring just to the boil, season and remove from the heat. Slice the steak on the diagonal and serve with the sauce immediately.

Variation For a vegetarian option, use a 51 g (1¾ oz) Quorn fillet instead of the beef, for 7 **ProPoints** values.

Curried Beef Skewers with Yogurt Dip

Marinating the beef in yogurt and spices not only adds flavour but tenderises the meat too.

Serves 4

2 tablespoons medium curry powder
300 g (10½ oz) 0% fat Greek yogurt
400 g (14 oz) beef escalope, cut into 1 cm (½ inch) thin strips
175 g (6 oz) dried couscous
200 ml (7 fl oz) boiling water
2 red peppers, de-seeded and cut into pieces
75 g (2¾ oz) frozen peas, defrosted
finely grated zest and juice of a lemon
2 garlic cloves, crushed
10 cm (4 inches) cucumber, de-seeded and chopped finely
3 tablespoons fresh mint, chopped
freshly ground black pepper

11 **ProPoints** values per serving
42 **ProPoints** values per recipe

C 447 **calories** per serving

Takes **25 minutes** to prepare + marinating and soaking

✱ not recommended

1 Place the curry powder in a small non stick saucepan and heat until hot. Stir for 1 minute before adding 2 tablespoons of water. Remove from the heat and leave to cool.

2 Add 4 tablespoons of the yogurt to the curry paste. Mix together, add the beef, cover and leave to marinate at room temperature for 20 minutes.

3 Meanwhile, place the couscous in a bowl and pour over enough boiling water to just cover. Cover with cling film and set aside to soak.

4 Preheat the grill to medium. Thread the beef on to metal skewers and grill for 10 minutes, turning regularly, until beginning to char.

5 Fluff the couscous up with a fork and stir in the peppers, peas and lemon zest and juice. Season with black pepper.

6 Mix together the remaining yogurt with the garlic, cucumber and mint. Serve the skewers on a mound of couscous with the yogurt on the side.

Tip You can use wooden skewers rather than metal ones, but make sure you soak them in water for 30 minutes before using to help prevent them from burning.

Variation You can try this recipe using the same weight of skinless boneless chicken breast, in place of the beef, for 9 **ProPoints** values per serving.

Lamb Dhansak

A mild, fragrant curry of lamb cooked with pumpkin, tomatoes and lentils.

Serves 4

1 teaspoon cumin seeds
2 large onions, chopped finely
150 g (5½ oz) canned chopped tomatoes
225 g (8 oz) pumpkin or butternut squash, peeled,
 de-seeded and chopped finely
a bunch of fresh coriander, chopped
a bunch of fresh mint, chopped
150 g (5½ oz) split yellow lentils
300 g (10½ oz) lean lamb, cubed
1 teaspoon turmeric
1 teaspoon chilli powder
1 teaspoon caster sugar
450 ml (16 fl oz) water
4 tablespoons vinegar
salt and freshly ground black pepper

1 Crush the cumin seeds using a pestle and mortar or the end of a rolling pin.

2 Put all the ingredients in a large pan, bring to the boil and then simmer for 1 hour or until the lentils and lamb are soft and tender.

3 Mash the lentils with a wooden spoon, taking care not to break up the meat, then serve.

7 ProPoints values per serving
30 ProPoints values per recipe

C **338 calories** per serving

Takes **30 minutes** to prepare,
1 hour to cook

✱ recommended

Spinach and Chick Pea Curry

Serves 2

300 g (10½ oz) baby new potatoes, scrubbed

calorie controlled cooking spray

1 onion, chopped

1 large garlic clove, crushed

1 teaspoon ginger purée (optional)

1–2 teaspoons mild or medium curry powder

140 g (5 oz) canned and drained chick peas

2 teaspoons plain flour

150 g tub very low fat natural bio yogurt

200 g packet baby spinach, washed

salt and freshly ground black pepper

1 Bring a pan of water to the boil, add the potatoes and cook for about 12 minutes, until just tender. Drain, cool and cut them into thick even slices.

2 Meanwhile, heat a medium lidded saucepan and spray it with the cooking spray. Add the onion, garlic, ginger purée (if using) and 4 tablespoons of water and cook until the mixture sizzles. Cover, reduce the heat and cook for 5 minutes until the onion has softened.

3 Add the curry powder, to taste, to the saucepan, with the sliced potatoes and chick peas. Cook for 1 minute. Stir the flour into the yogurt and add to the pan. Heat gently until the sauce thickens.

4 Next, gradually stir in the spinach leaves until they have all wilted and are thoroughly mixed in. Check the seasoning and serve.

(C) **9 ProPoints** values per serving
17 ProPoints values per recipe

C **356 calories** per serving

⊙ Takes **12 minutes** to prepare, **15 minutes** to cook

V

✱ recommended

Chilli Chicken with Flageolet Beans

Baking everything in one roasting tin preserves all the delicious juices. Serve with a simple zero *ProPoints* value green salad.

Serves 2

calorie controlled cooking spray
2 x 150 g (5½ oz) skinless boneless chicken
  breasts
2 garlic cloves, sliced
6 tomatoes on the vine, vine removed
410 g can flageolet beans, drained and rinsed
2 tablespoons balsamic vinegar
2 teaspoons chilli flakes

---

6 *ProPoints* values per serving
13 *ProPoints* values per recipe

307 calories per serving

Takes **10 minutes** to prepare,
25 minutes to cook

✱ not recommended

1 Preheat the oven to Gas Mark 6/200°C/fan oven 180°C. Lightly spray a non stick frying pan with the cooking spray and heat until hot. Add the chicken breasts and fry for 3–4 minutes until golden on both sides.

2 Mix together the remaining ingredients and tip into a roasting tin with 2 tablespoons of water. Place the chicken breasts on top, pushing them down slightly so that they nestle in the beans.

3 Cook for 25 minutes until the chicken is tender and cooked through.

Tip Try this with skinless boneless duck breasts instead of chicken, for 8 *ProPoints* values per serving.

Lamb Jalfrezi

This tastes really authentic, making it a real treat for a Friday night instead of a takeaway.

Serves 4

400 g (14 oz) lean stewing lamb (neck fillet), trimmed of visible fat and diced
1 teaspoon cumin seeds
2 teaspoons sunflower oil
1 onion, sliced thinly
2 garlic cloves, chopped finely
2 cm (¾ inch) fresh root ginger, grated
1 large green chilli, de-seeded and chopped
1 teaspoon paprika
½ teaspoon hot chilli powder
½ teaspoon ground turmeric
1 red pepper, de-seeded and sliced
1 small yellow pepper, de-seeded and sliced
4 tomatoes, skinned and chopped
150 ml (5 fl oz) vegetable stock
2 tablespoons chopped fresh coriander
salt and freshly ground black pepper

8 *ProPoints* values per serving
34 *ProPoints* values per recipe

C 360 calories per serving

Takes 30 minutes to prepare,
50 minutes to cook

* recommended

1 Preheat the oven to Gas Mark 4/180°C/fan oven 160°C. Heat a large non stick frying pan and brown the lamb on all sides for about 5 minutes. You will need to do this in batches. Transfer to a medium, lidded, ovenproof casserole dish.

2 Sprinkle the cumin seeds into the frying pan and cook for a few seconds to release their aroma. Add the oil, onion, garlic, ginger and chilli. Stir and cook gently for 3 minutes. Mix in the paprika, hot chilli powder and turmeric. Cook for another minute.

3 Add the peppers and tomatoes and continue cooking for 5 minutes until they have softened. Add the stock towards the end of the 5 minutes. Season well then pour the sauce over the lamb.

4 Put the lid on the casserole dish and bake for about 50 minutes or until the lamb is tender. Stir in the coriander before serving.

Quorn and Chick Pea Tikka

This filling and flavoursome recipe is the perfect alternative to chicken tikka.

Serves 4

2 carrots, peeled and chopped

¼ Savoy cabbage, shredded

100 g (3½ oz) green beans, topped, tailed and each cut into 3 pieces

calorie controlled cooking spray

1 large onion, chopped

200 g (7 oz) mushrooms, sliced

150 g (5½ oz) Quorn pieces

200 g (7 oz) frozen sweetcorn or canned sweetcorn, drained

400 g can chick peas, drained and rinsed

400 g can chopped tomatoes

150 ml (5 fl oz) vegetable stock

2 tablespoons tikka curry powder

salt and freshly ground black pepper

5 ProPoints values per serving
21 ProPoints values per recipe

C **247 calories** per serving

Takes **15 minutes** to prepare,
45 minutes to cook

V

✱ recommended

1 Bring a pan of water to the boil, add the carrots, cabbage and beans and simmer for 10–15 minutes, until just soft. Drain and set aside.

2 Meanwhile spray a large, lidded, non stick frying pan or wok with the cooking spray. Fry the onion for a few minutes until soft, adding a tablespoon or more of water if it begins to stick.

3 Add the mushrooms and Quorn pieces to the onion and stir fry for 4–5 minutes. Add all the other ingredients to the pan including the carrots, cabbage and beans.

4 Stir together, and then cover and cook on a low heat for 25 minutes, stirring from time to time. Remove the lid for the last 10 minutes, turning up the heat to reduce the liquid a little and to make a rich curry.

Variations Any zero **ProPoints** value vegetable can be used in this dish.

Haricot beans, kidney beans, butterbeans or lentils can be substituted for the chick peas. Remember to adjust the **ProPoints** values accordingly.

Tandoori Chicken

Tandoor is actually the name of the clay oven that is used to cook this dish, but it will taste just as good cooked in a normal oven.

Serves 2

2 x 165 g (5¾ oz) skinless boneless chicken breasts, cut in half
½ teaspoon salt
1 tablespoon lemon juice

For the marinade

185 g (6½ oz) low fat natural yogurt
½ small onion, chopped
½ garlic clove, chopped
1 teaspoon chopped fresh root ginger
½ green chilli, de-seeded and chopped
1 teaspoon garam masala

For the raita

½ cucumber, grated
100 g (3½ oz) low fat natural yogurt
1 tablespoon chopped fresh mint leaves

To serve

shredded Iceberg lettuce
2 tomatoes, sliced

---

6 ProPoints values per serving
13 ProPoints values per recipe

333 calories per serving

Takes **25 minutes** to prepare + marinating, **20–25 minutes** to cook

✳ not recommended

1 Make two slits in each of the four pieces of chicken and lay the chicken pieces on a large plate. Sprinkle with half the salt and half the lemon juice and then turn the pieces over and repeat with the remaining salt and lemon juice. Leave to stand for 15 minutes.

2 Place all the marinade ingredients in a food processor, or use a hand held blender, and blend until smooth.

3 Place the chicken and any leftover juices into a bowl and pour over the marinade. Rub the marinade into the slits of the chicken and then cover and leave to marinate in the fridge for as long as you can – between 5–8 hours is ideal.

4 Preheat the oven to its hottest temperature and place a shelf near the top.

5 Spread the chicken pieces on a non stick baking tray and bake for 20–25 minutes, until cooked through. The juices should run clear when the thickest part is pierced with a skewer.

6 For the raita, mix together the cucumber, yogurt and mint and serve with the chicken, along with the shredded lettuce and sliced tomatoes.

Variation Turkey breasts or pork fillets can be prepared in exactly the same way. The **ProPoints** values will then be 6 and 8 per serving respectively.

Aubergine Madras

A mild curry that makes a satisfying supper for one. It's also a great accompaniment for grilled meat or fish.

Serves 1

1 aubergine, cut in half lengthways
1 teaspoon curry paste
calorie controlled cooking spray
1 small onion, sliced thinly
2 garlic cloves, sliced thinly
½ teaspoon ground cumin
½ teaspoon ground coriander
½ teaspoon garam masala
100 ml (3½ fl oz) vegetable stock
2 tablespoons low fat natural yogurt
2 tablespoons chopped fresh coriander, plus extra sprigs to garnish
salt and freshly ground black pepper

3 *ProPoints* values per serving
3 *ProPoints* values per recipe

C **200 calories** per serving

Takes **35 minutes**

V

✱ not recommended

1 Preheat the oven to Gas Mark 4/180°C/fan oven 160°C. Score the exposed flesh of the aubergine halves with a sharp knife in a deep criss cross fashion and then spread the curry paste over. Place the halves, cut side up, on a baking tray. Bake for 20 minutes, until softened.

2 Meanwhile, heat a non stick frying pan, spray with the cooking spray and stir fry the onion and garlic for 5 minutes, until softened, adding a tablespoon of water, if necessary, to prevent them from sticking. Add the spices, fry for another minute then turn off the heat.

3 When the aubergine is cooked, transfer it to a board and chop it into cubes as marked by the score lines. Add it to the onion mixture, with the stock, and bring to the boil. Boil rapidly, without a lid, for 10 minutes, until the curry is nearly dry.

4 Take off the heat, stir in the yogurt and chopped coriander, season and serve, garnished with the coriander sprigs.

Spicy Veggie Balls in Kefta Sauce

3 ProPoints value

These spicy meatballs are great for a weekend family supper.

Serves 4

1 large red onion, chopped finely
150 ml (5 fl oz) hot vegetable stock
225 g (8 oz) Quorn mince
1 tablespoon chopped fresh mint
1 tablespoon chopped fresh parsley
½ teaspoon dried marjoram
75 g (2¾ oz) fresh breadcrumbs
1 egg, beaten
¼ teaspoon ground cumin
¼ teaspoon cayenne pepper
¼ teaspoon paprika
¼ teaspoon mixed spice
salt and freshly ground black pepper

For the sauce

3 x 400 g cans chopped tomatoes
1 red onion, chopped finely
1 tablespoon chopped fresh parsley
1 garlic clove, crushed
300 ml (10 fl oz) water
a pinch of salt, paprika and cayenne pepper

---

3 ProPoints values per serving
12 ProPoints values per recipe

C **190 calories** per serving

🕒 Takes **1¼ hours**

V

✱ not recommended

1 To make the kefta sauce, put all the sauce ingredients into a large saucepan, heat and simmer gently for 1 hour–1 hour 10 minutes.

2 Meanwhile, make the veggie balls. Heat a non stick saucepan, add the onion and stock and simmer for 10 minutes, or until the liquid has just evaporated. Tip into a mixing bowl and allow to cool. Preheat the oven to Gas Mark 4/180°C/fan oven 160°C.

3 Add all the remaining ingredients to the onion. Stir well to combine, then shape into 12 golf ball size balls. Arrange in a roasting tin or ovenproof baking dish in a single layer. Roast in the oven for 25–30 minutes, or until browned and crispy on the outside.

4 Put the cooked veggie balls into the sauce and simmer for 5 minutes before serving.

Seafood Goan Curry

Goa is a state on the west coast of India where fish and seafood is what the locals thrive on. This recipe uses some of the wonderful spices available there.

Serves 4

110 g (4 oz) dried basmati rice
1 teaspoon paprika
1 teaspoon cayenne pepper
¼ teaspoon turmeric
1 tablespoon ground coriander
1 teaspoon ground cumin
1 tablespoon lemon juice
½ teaspoon salt
calorie controlled cooking spray
½ teaspoon mustard seeds
1 onion, chopped
2 garlic cloves, sliced
200 ml (7 fl oz) reduced fat coconut milk
350 g (12 oz) mixed seafood
a bunch of fresh coriander, chopped, to garnish

6 ProPoints values per serving
25 ProPoints values per recipe

C 245 calories per serving

Takes **10 minutes** to prepare,
20 minutes to cook

✳ not recommended

1 Bring a pan of water to the boil, add the rice and cook according to packet instructions.

2 In a small bowl, mix together the paprika, cayenne pepper, turmeric, coriander, cumin and lemon juice. Add the salt and 1 tablespoon of water to the bowl and set to one side.

3 Heat a non stick frying pan and spray with the cooking spray. Add the mustard seeds and, when they start popping, add the onion and garlic. Cook for 4–5 minutes until they start to turn golden.

4 Pour in the spice mixture and cook for 1–2 minutes, stirring.

5 Pour the coconut milk into the pan and simmer for 4–5 minutes. Add the seafood and simmer for another 3–4 minutes. Sprinkle over the coriander and serve with the basmati rice.

Variation For a prawn curry, substitute the same weight of prawns for the seafood. The **ProPoints** values per serving will remain the same.

Beef Rhogan Josh

This medium spiced curry thickens up beautifully while cooking. Don't be put off by the length of cooking time – you can actually walk away and let it cook on its own.

Serves 2

calorie controlled cooking spray
200 g (7 oz) lean braising steak, cubed
1 onion, sliced
1 green pepper, de-seeded and sliced
4 cm (1½ inch) fresh root ginger, grated
2 garlic cloves, crushed
1 teaspoon crushed chilli flakes
4 cardamom pods, seeds only
2 teaspoons ground cumin
2 teaspoons turmeric
2 teaspoons ground coriander
3 tablespoons low fat natural yogurt
400 g can chopped tomatoes

6 **ProPoints** values per serving
12 **ProPoints** values per recipe

C 350 **calories** per serving

Takes **25 minutes** to prepare,
1 hour to cook

V

✱ not recommended

1 Lightly coat a large, lidded, non stick pan with the cooking spray and heat until hot. Add the steak and cook for 3–4 minutes until browned all over. You may need to do this in batches. Remove from the pan and set aside.

2 Spray the pan again, add the onion and pepper and stir fry for 5 minutes until beginning to brown.

3 Add the ginger, garlic and spices. Cook for a further minute before adding the yogurt, tomatoes and finally the steak.

4 Stir in 300 ml (10 fl oz) of water, bring to the boil, cover and reduce the heat. Leave to simmer for 1 hour until the meat is tender.

Pork Curry with Lime

This very tasty curry is easy to make; all the ingredients are put in a pot and left to cook.

Serves 4

1 tablespoon Thai green curry paste
400 g (14 oz) lean pork fillet, cubed
2 tablespoons plain flour
4 garlic cloves, chopped
grated zest and juice of a lime
300 g (10½ oz) potatoes, peeled and diced
4 tomatoes, chopped
leaves from a rosemary sprig, chopped
300 ml (10 fl oz) stock
2 tablespoons Worcestershire sauce
150 ml (5 fl oz) virtually fat free fromage frais
salt and freshly ground black pepper

1 Preheat the oven to Gas Mark 4/180°C/fan oven 160°C. Heat a lidded flameproof and ovenproof casserole dish then add the curry paste and pork and toss until browned all over and coated in the curry paste. Add the flour and seasoning and toss again.

2 Add all the other ingredients except the fromage frais and put in the oven, covered, for 2 hours.

3 When cooked, take out of the oven, stir in the fromage frais and serve.

7 ProPoints values per serving
28 ProPoints values per recipe

302 calories per serving

Takes **20 minutes** to prepare, **2 hours** to cook

✳ not recommended

Turkey Steaks with Korma Rice

Serves 2

2 x 100 g (3½ oz) turkey steaks
grated zest and juice of a lime
calorie controlled cooking spray
1 onion, chopped finely
1 heaped teaspoon korma spice
  blend
100 g (3½ oz) dried long grain
  rice

125 ml (4 fl oz) Chinese cooking
  wine
250 ml (9 fl oz) vegetable stock
2 eggs
30 g (1¼ oz) raisins
150 g (5½ oz) baby spinach, rinsed
salt and freshly ground black
  pepper

1 Put the turkey steaks into a shallow non metallic dish and coat in the lime zest and juice. Heat a wide, lidded, non stick pan and spray with the cooking spray. Cook the onion for 3–4 minutes until softened. Stir in the korma spices, rice and cooking wine and bubble rapidly for 1 minute. Add the stock, bring to the boil, cover and simmer for 12–15 minutes until tender.

2 Meanwhile, put the eggs into a pan of water, bring to the boil and simmer for 5 minutes, then plunge into cold water. When the rice is cooked, stir in the raisins and spinach, cover and keep on a low heat, stirring occasionally until the spinach wilts. Season.

3 Meanwhile, heat a griddle or non stick frying pan until hot. Spray with the cooking spray and cook the turkey for 10 minutes, turning halfway. Peel and halve the eggs and serve with the rice and steaks.

13 ProPoints values per serving
27 ProPoints values per recipe

C **529 calories** per serving

Takes **45 minutes**

✱ not recommended

Nasi Goreng

Nasi goreng means 'fried rice' and usually consists of rice with eggs, prawns and other ingredients.

Serves 4

240 g (8½ oz) dried white rice
4 teaspoons Indonesian or Thai red curry paste
a bunch of spring onions, chopped
4 garlic cloves, sliced finely
200 g (7 oz) cooked, peeled prawns, defrosted if frozen
2 tablespoons soy sauce
200 g (7 oz) frozen petit pois
1 tablespoon fish sauce
juice of a lime
2 eggs, beaten
a small bunch of coriander, chopped, to garnish

10 *ProPoints* values per serving
41 *ProPoints* values per recipe

387 calories per serving

Takes **20 minutes**

not recommended

1 Bring a pan of water to the boil, add the rice and cook according to packet instructions, then drain.

2 Heat the curry paste in a large non stick wok or frying pan and add the spring onions and garlic. Stir fry for 4–5 minutes, until softened.

3 Add the remaining ingredients, except the eggs and coriander but including the rice, and stir fry for 5 minutes. Now push everything to one side of the wok or pan and tip the eggs into the gap. Stir them until set, like scrambled egg, then stir into the other ingredients from the side of the wok or pan.

4 Scatter with the chopped coriander and serve.

Lamb Kofta Curry

Koftas are meatballs very popular in the Middle East, Asia and India.

Serves 4

For the meatballs
1 onion, quartered
2 garlic cloves, peeled
2 green chillies, de-seeded and chopped
2.5 cm (1 inch) fresh root ginger, sliced
1 tablespoon chopped fresh coriander, plus extra
 to garnish
½ teaspoon ground cumin
350 g (12 oz) extra lean lamb mince
50 g (1¾ oz) fresh breadcrumbs
salt and freshly ground black pepper

For the curry sauce
2 teaspoons sunflower oil
1 onion, chopped finely
2 tablespoons medium curry powder
1 teaspoon cumin seeds
½ teaspoon hot chilli powder
400 g can chopped tomatoes
150 ml (5 fl oz) vegetable stock
100 g (3½ oz) low fat natural yogurt

8 *ProPoints* values per serving
31 *ProPoints* values per recipe

C   331 **calories** per serving

Takes **20 minutes** to prepare + **30 minutes**
chilling, **30 minutes** to cook

✻   not recommended

1 To make the meatballs, whizz the onion, garlic, chillies, ginger and the 1 tablespoon of chopped coriander together in a food processor until finely chopped. Add the ground cumin, lamb mince, breadcrumbs and seasoning and pulse together until just mixed.

2 Shape into 20 small meatballs then chill, covered, for 30 minutes.

3 For the sauce, heat a large, lidded, non stick pan, add the oil and onion and soften the onion for 3 minutes.

4 Add the spices and cook for 30 seconds before stirring in the tomatoes and stock. Season and bring to a simmer, then gradually stir in the yogurt.

5 Slide in the chilled meatballs and gently push them down into the sauce. Cover and simmer gently for 30 minutes, shaking the pan from time to time to move the meatballs around. Serve garnished with the chopped fresh coriander.

Tip The meatballs firm up when chilled, which makes them less likely to break up in the sauce.

Variation You can substitute extra lean beef mince or turkey mince for the lamb if you prefer, the *ProPoints* values will be 7 and 6 respectively.

Creamy Cauliflower and Potato Curry

An unlikely sounding recipe, but this is a case where the finished dish is so much more than the sum of its parts. The milk and tomato purée combine in this curry to give a silky textured spicy sauce, the flavour of which is taken on by the vegetables.

Serves 2

calorie controlled cooking spray
1 onion, chopped
1 teaspoon cumin seeds
¼ teaspoon ground turmeric
a pinch of hot chilli powder
2 tablespoons tomato purée
200 g (7 oz) potatoes, peeled and diced
200 g (7 oz) cauliflower, broken into florets
3 tomatoes, chopped roughly
150 ml (5 fl oz) skimmed milk
salt and freshly ground black pepper
2 tablespoons chopped fresh coriander, to garnish

---

3 ProPoints values per serving
7 ProPoints values per recipe

207 calories per serving

Takes **10 minutes** to prepare,
15 minutes to cook

V

✻ not recommended

1 Heat a large, lidded, non stick pan, spray with the cooking spray and cook the onion for 3 minutes over a high heat until browned, adding a splash of water if it starts to stick. Stir in the cumin seeds and cook for 30 seconds.

2 Add the turmeric, chilli powder and tomato purée, then mix in the potatoes and cauliflower to coat in the spice paste.

3 Add the tomatoes, milk, 3 tablespoons of cold water and seasoning. Bring to a simmer, cover and cook for 10 minutes.

4 Remove the lid and cook for 5 minutes to reduce the sauce slightly. Serve with the coriander leaves scattered over the curry.

Chilli Con Carne

With more vegetables and a little less meat than usual, this chilli is absolutely delicious.

Serves 4

350 g (12 oz) very lean beef mince
1 large onion, chopped
2 garlic cloves, crushed
1 courgette, chopped finely
1 large carrot, peeled and chopped finely
1 red or green pepper, de-seeded and chopped
2–3 teaspoons medium chilli powder
400 g can chopped tomatoes
2 tablespoons tomato purée
400 g can red kidney beans, drained and rinsed
300 ml (10 fl oz) beef or vegetable stock
200 g (7 oz) dried long grain rice
a kettleful of boiling water
salt and freshly ground black pepper

11 *ProPoints* values per serving
43 *ProPoints* values per recipe

C **457 calories** per serving

Takes **10 minutes** to prepare,
40 minutes to cook

★ recommended

1 Heat a large, lidded, non stick saucepan and add the mince, a handful at a time, so that it seals and browns.

2 Add the onion, garlic, courgette, carrot, pepper, chilli powder, tomatoes, tomato purée, kidney beans and stock. Stir well and bring to the boil. Cover and reduce the heat. Simmer for about 30 minutes, stirring from time to time.

3 Fifteen minutes before you're ready to serve, bring a pan of water to the boil and cook the rice according to the packet instructions. Drain well and rinse with boiling water.

4 Check the seasoning of the chilli. Divide the cooked rice between four warm serving plates and pile the chilli on top. Serve at once.

Tip Remember to cook spicy food according to your taste. Add more chilli powder or use a hotter variety if you like things spicy. Use less or a milder type if you prefer less heat.

Variations For a vegetarian version, use 350 g (12 oz) of Quorn mince instead of the beef mince and use vegetable stock. The *ProPoints* values per serving will be 9.

For a change, omit the rice and fill eight soft flour tortillas with the chilli instead. Bake at Gas Mark 5/190°C/fan oven 170°C for 20 minutes, or until the tortillas are light brown and crispy. Serve with shredded lettuce, onion, cucumber and tomato. The *ProPoints* values per serving will be 13.

Fruity Pork Curry

The whole family will love this classic combination of pork and pineapple. Serve with a generous portion of stir fried zero *ProPoints* value vegetables

Serves 4

1 small onion, chopped finely

1 lemongrass stem, tough outer leaves discarded and chopped

25 g packet fresh coriander, chopped

450 g (1 lb) lean pork loin steak, visible fat removed and cubed

2 tablespoons medium curry powder

calorie controlled cooking spray

1 red or green pepper, de-seeded and diced

200 ml (7 fl oz) hot chicken stock

300 g (10½ oz) passata

4 fresh or canned pineapple rings in natural juice, drained and cut into pieces

---

6 *ProPoints* values per serving
22 *ProPoints* values per recipe

C   265 calories per serving

Takes **18 minutes**

✱   recommended

1 Put the onion, lemongrass and coriander into a food processor and whizz until finely chopped. Transfer to a bowl and add the pork and curry powder. Mix to coat the pork in the spices.

2 Heat a wide non stick saucepan and spray with the cooking spray. Add the pork and pepper and cook for 5 minutes, stirring. Add the stock, passata and pineapple. Simmer for 5 minutes until the pork is cooked and the sauce is thickened. Serve immediately.

Cumin Lamb with Spinach Dhal

Serve with 100 g (3½ oz) of green beans per person, for no additional **ProPoints** values.

Serves 4

150 g (5½ oz) dried red lentils, rinsed
1 onion, chopped finely
2 teaspoons curry powder
3 teaspoons cumin seeds
600 ml (20 fl oz) boiling water
410 g can pinto beans, drained and rinsed
4 x 100 g (3½ oz) lean lamb leg steaks, visible
 fat removed
calorie controlled cooking spray
100 g (3½ oz) young leaf spinach, washed
freshly ground black pepper

10 ProPoints values per serving
40 ProPoints values per recipe

C **392 calories** per serving

Takes **30 minutes**

✱ not recommended

1 To make the dhal, place the lentils, onion, curry powder and
1 teaspoon of cumin seeds in a lidded non stick saucepan with the
boiling water. Cover and bring back to the boil then simmer for
15 minutes. Stir in the pinto beans, re-cover the pan and cook for a
further 5 minutes.

2 Meanwhile, lightly season the lamb steaks with freshly ground black
pepper and press the remaining 2 teaspoons of cumin seeds on to
the meat. Heat a non stick frying pan, spray with the cooking spray
and cook the lamb for 3–4 minutes on each side over a high heat
until cooked to your liking.

3 Stir the spinach into the pan of lentils until wilted. Ladle the dhal on
to serving plates and serve with the lamb.

Chicken Korma

A real favourite – this is rich and creamy but still low in *ProPoints* values.

Serves 4

6 garlic cloves, chopped
4 cm (1½ inch) fresh root ginger, chopped
2 tablespoons chicken stock
calorie controlled cooking spray
1 onion, diced finely
1 bay leaf
8 cardamom pods, cracked
4 cloves
2.5 cm (1 inch) cinnamon stick
1 tablespoon ground cumin
1 tablespoon ground coriander
¼ teaspoon cayenne pepper
1 tablespoon tomato purée
600 g (1 lb 5 oz) skinless boneless chicken
  breast, cut into bite size pieces
3 tablespoons low fat fromage frais
3 tablespoons low fat natural yogurt
150 ml (5 fl oz) chicken stock
2 teaspoons garam masala

---

6 *ProPoints* values per serving
26 *ProPoints* values per recipe

C **275 calories** per serving

Takes **20 minutes** to prepare,
55 minutes to cook

✱ recommended (for up to 1 month)

1 Place the garlic, ginger and chicken stock in a blender, or use a hand held blender, and whizz to a paste.

2 Heat a large non stick frying pan, spray with the cooking spray and add the onion, bay leaf, cardamom pods, cloves and cinnamon stick. Cook for 3–4 minutes, stirring occasionally.

3 Add the cumin, coriander, cayenne pepper and tomato purée. Stir to combine. Stir in the chicken to coat with all the spices.

4 Stir in the remaining ingredients and bring to a simmer for 25 minutes or until the chicken is cooked through.

Monkfish and Coconut Curry

This deliciously fragrant curry is quick and easy to make, and great for both special occasions and family suppers.

Serves 4

calorie controlled cooking spray

2 onions, chopped roughly

400 g (14 oz) monkfish tails, cut into bite size pieces

2 tablespoons Thai green curry paste

175 g (6 oz) green beans, cut into 2.5 cm (1 inch) lengths

225 g (8 oz) peas, fresh or frozen

225 g (8 oz) courgettes, cut into 2.5 cm (1 inch) batons

400 g can chopped tomatoes

40 g (1½ oz) creamed coconut

250 g (9 oz) dried egg noodles

25 g packet fresh coriander or basil, chopped roughly

salt and freshly ground black pepper

---

12 *ProPoints* values per serving
48 *ProPoints* values per recipe

C **502 calories** per serving

Takes **5 minutes** to prepare, **35 minutes** to cook

✱ recommended

1 Heat a large frying pan or wok and spray with the cooking spray. Add the onions and cook until soft – about 4 minutes, adding a splash of water if they start to stick, then add the monkfish and curry paste and stir fry for 2 minutes.

2 Add the beans, peas, courgettes, tomatoes, creamed coconut, 300 ml (10 fl oz) of water and seasoning. Cook for 25 minutes, stirring occasionally.

3 While the curry is cooking, bring a large pan of water to the boil, add the noodles and cook according to the packet instructions. Drain and keep warm.

4 Check the seasoning of the curry and add the coriander or basil. Serve with the noodles.

Chicken Tikka Kebabs

If you can leave the chicken to marinate overnight, it will become even more succulent and full of flavour.

Serves 2

1 tablespoon hot curry powder
¼ teaspoon turmeric
1 garlic clove, crushed
1 teaspoon grated fresh root ginger
1 tablespoon lemon juice
100 ml (3½ fl oz) low fat natural yogurt
2 x 150 g (5½ oz) skinless boneless chicken
  breasts
1 green pepper, de-seeded and cut into chunks
1 red onion, cut into chunks
salt and freshly ground black pepper

5 ProPoints values per serving
10 ProPoints values per recipe

C 249 calories per serving

Takes **15 minutes** to prepare + **30 minutes** marinating, **15 minutes** to cook

V

✱ recommended for up to **1 month**

1 Mix the spices, garlic, ginger, lemon juice, yogurt and seasoning together until smooth. Cut each chicken breast into seven or eight pieces and toss in the yogurt mixture to coat. Cover and chill for at least 30 minutes.

2 Preheat the grill to its highest setting or prepare your barbecue. Thread the marinated chicken on to four short skewers, alternating with pieces of pepper and onion.

3 Grill or barbecue the kebabs for 15 minutes, turning occasionally, until the chicken is cooked through and slightly charred at the edges.

Tips If you want to achieve the reddish colour of chicken tikka that is found in restaurants where colouring is used, leave the turmeric out of the marinade and add ½ teaspoon of paprika plus 1 tablespoon of tomato purée. The **ProPoints** values will remain the same.

Soak wooden skewers in water for 30 minutes before using to prevent them from burning.

Variation For vegetarian tikka kebabs, marinate 16 button mushrooms in the tikka marinade instead of the chicken. These kebabs will take only 8–10 minutes to cook and will be just 1 **ProPoints** value per serving.

Chicken Biryani

Biryani, which originated from Persia, is a rice dish, usually served with a curry.

Serves 4

calorie controlled cooking spray
4 cloves
4 cm (1½ inch) cinnamon stick
2 garlic cloves, peeled
4 cm (1½ inch) fresh root ginger, finely grated
300 g (10½ oz) dried brown basmati rice, washed
300 g (10½ oz) skinless boneless chicken breasts, cut into bite size pieces
150 g (5½ oz) low fat natural yogurt
½ teaspoon cumin seeds, ground
1 teaspoon ground turmeric
2 onions, chopped
400 g can chopped tomatoes
2 teaspoons garam masala
salt and freshly ground black pepper
a small bunch of fresh coriander, chopped, to garnish (optional)

10 ProPoints values per serving
40 ProPoints values per recipe

C **426 calories** per serving

Takes **20 minutes** to prepare,
1 hour 30 minutes to cook

✱ not recommended

1. Heat a large, lidded, non stick saucepan, spray with the cooking spray and cook the cloves, cinnamon, garlic and ginger for 1 minute. Add the rice and 850 ml (1½ pints) of water. Bring to the boil and then simmer for 30 minutes, until most of the water has been absorbed. Cover and cook for a further 5 minutes, then turn off the heat.

2. Meanwhile, mix the chicken with the yogurt, seasoning, cumin and turmeric and set aside. Heat a large non stick frying pan and spray with the cooking spray. Fry the onions for 4 minutes and then add the tomatoes and garam masala. Bring to boil and simmer for 10 minutes.

3. Add the chicken mixture with 150 ml (5 fl oz) of hot water. Bring to the boil and simmer for 15 minutes, until the sauce is thick and the chicken cooked through.

4. Preheat the oven to Gas Mark 6/200°C/fan oven 180°C. Layer the chicken in a deep ovenproof dish with the cooked rice, finishing with a rice layer. Bake for 10 minutes.

5. Serve sprinkled with the fresh coriander, if using.

Beef and Pea Keema

This is a quick and tasty Indian style dish of beef and peas.

Serves 4

calorie controlled cooking spray
500 g (1 lb 2 oz) extra lean beef mince
2 large garlic cloves, chopped
a bunch of spring onions, chopped
2–3 teaspoons mild or medium curry powder
1 tablespoon mango chutney
1 tablespoon plain flour
300 ml (10 fl oz) beef stock
125 g (4½ oz) frozen peas
salt and freshly ground black pepper

To serve

150 g (5½ oz) low fat natural yogurt
1–2 tablespoons chopped fresh coriander
  or parsley

---

8 *ProPoints* values per serving
33 *ProPoints* values per recipe

C 318 **calories** per serving

Takes **5 minutes** to prepare,
20 minutes to cook

✱ recommended (see Tip)

1 Heat a non stick wok or large frying pan. When you can feel a good heat rising, spray the pan with the cooking spray. Add the mince in small amounts, stirring quickly to break it up. Cook until the meat is browned and crumbly.

2 Add the garlic and spring onions and cook for 2 minutes. Stir in the curry powder and cook for 1 minute.

3 Mix in the mango chutney and flour and then slowly stir in the stock. Season and bring to the boil while stirring. Reduce the heat and simmer for 10 minutes.

4 Add the peas to the pan and cook for 3 more minutes. Serve hot, topped with the yogurt and chopped coriander or parsley.

Tip When freezing this dish, omit the yogurt and fresh herbs.

Variations Try making this dish with turkey mince instead of beef. The *ProPoints* values will then be 7 per serving.

For a vegetarian alternative, replace the beef mince with the same quantity of Quorn mince. The *ProPoints* values will be 6 per serving.

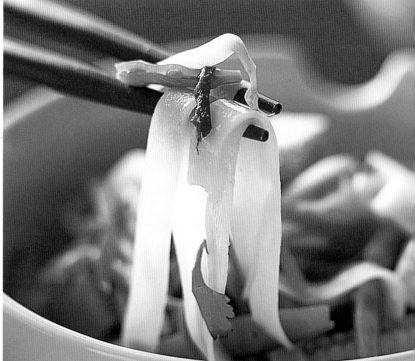

Far Eastern Favourites

From traditional Thai dishes, such as Chicken Pad Thai, to Chinese favourites, including Chinese Meatballs, Chicken and Mango Stir Fry and Teriyaki Noodles, your whole family will love these fabulous Far Eastern dishes.

Fresh and zingy, these recipes will liven up your mealtimes

Eastern Spiced Chicken

Star anise infuses this dish with a wonderful aniseed flavour. Spoon the chicken on top of 150 g (5½ oz) of cooked straight to wok udon noodles per person and stir fried zero **ProPoints** value vegetables, for an additional 6 **ProPoints** values per serving.

Serves 4

600 g (1 lb 5 oz) skinless boneless chicken breast, cut into even chunks

1 teaspoon ground cinnamon

calorie controlled cooking spray

2 tablespoons tomato purée

250 ml (9 fl oz) hot chicken stock

4 tablespoons dark soy sauce

100 ml (3½ fl oz) mature balsamic vinegar

1 cm (½ inch) fresh root ginger, sliced into matchsticks

2 star anise

1 wide strip of pared orange zest

4 spring onions, sliced diagonally into short lengths

5 **ProPoints** values per serving
20 **ProPoints** values per recipe

278 **calories** per serving

Takes **25 minutes**

* recommended

1 Put the chicken chunks into a bowl and coat in the cinnamon. Heat a wide non stick saucepan and spray with the cooking spray. Cook the chicken for 5 minutes, stirring until browned. Add the tomato purée then gradually stir in the stock, soy sauce and balsamic vinegar.

2 Add the ginger, star anise and orange zest. Gently bubble for 8 minutes. Add the spring onions and simmer for 2 minutes until cooked and the sauce is reduced. Serve immediately.

Teriyaki Noodles

Rice noodles are sold dried and need to be soaked before use – just follow the packet directions.

Serves 2

2 tablespoons teriyaki sauce or dark soy sauce

1 tablespoon lime or lemon juice

1–2 teaspoons chilli sauce, according to taste

1 tablespoon chopped fresh coriander

225 g (8 oz) firm tofu, cubed

100 g (3½ oz) dried rice noodles

1 teaspoon stir fry oil or sesame oil

1 garlic clove, crushed

250 g (9 oz) zero *ProPoints* value fresh or frozen stir fry vegetables

60 g (2 oz) beansprouts

salt and freshly ground black pepper

a handful of spring onions, shredded into fine strips, to garnish

9 *ProPoints* values per serving
19 *ProPoints* values per recipe

410 calories per serving

Takes **20 minutes** + **1 hour** marinating

V

* not recommended

1 Mix together the teriyaki sauce or soy sauce, lime or lemon juice, chilli sauce and coriander in a non metallic bowl. Add the tofu cubes, stir well, cover and refrigerate for at least 1 hour.

2 When ready to cook, put the noodles into a large bowl and cover them with warm water. Leave them to soak for about 5 minutes, or follow the packet instructions, then drain well.

3 Heat the stir fry oil or sesame oil in a non stick wok or large frying pan. Add the garlic and vegetables (but not the beansprouts) and stir fry them over a high heat for 2–3 minutes.

4 Add the noodles to the wok or frying pan and cook, stirring, for another 2 minutes. Now add the beansprouts and tofu with its marinade.

5 Cook over a medium-high heat, stirring gently, for 1–2 minutes until all the ingredients are heated through. Check the seasoning, adding more to taste, and then serve garnished with the spring onions.

Variation Use 225 g (8 oz) of peeled prawns instead of the tofu, if you prefer. The *ProPoints* values per serving will remain the same.

Thai Beef Curry

9 ProPoints value

This spicy little number is a fantastic winter warmer.

Serves 4

300 ml (10 fl oz) reduced fat coconut milk
2 tablespoons Thai red curry paste
1 lemongrass stem, sliced thinly
4 dried or fresh kaffir lime leaves
1 tablespoon fresh lime juice
1 tablespoon Thai fish sauce
450 g (1 lb) lean rump steak, trimmed of visible
   fat and sliced thinly
225 g (8 oz) shallots
150 g (5½ oz) carrots, peeled and sliced thinly
175 g (6 oz) sugarsnap peas
175 g (6 oz) cherry tomatoes, halved
3 tablespoons chopped fresh coriander

9 *ProPoints* values per serving
37 *ProPoints* values per recipe

C **398 calories** per serving

Takes **40 minutes**

* recommended

1 Place the coconut milk in a large saucepan with 300 ml (10 fl oz) of water. Add the curry paste, lemongrass, kaffir lime leaves, lime juice and fish sauce and bring to the boil. Boil rapidly for 2 minutes.

2 Add the steak and shallots to the pan and simmer for 10 minutes. Add the carrots and sugarsnap peas and cook for a further 10 minutes.

3 Stir in the cherry tomatoes and chopped coriander and heat them through for 2 minutes. Serve the curry ladled into warmed bowls.

Glazed Oriental Salmon

A chic and stylish dinner that tastes as fantastic as it looks.

Serves 4

4 cm (1½ inch) fresh root ginger, chopped finely
4 garlic cloves, chopped finely
75 ml (3 fl oz) oyster sauce
1 tablespoon sweet chilli sauce
2 tablespoons soy sauce, plus extra to serve
4 x 150 g (5½ oz) salmon fillets
4 heads of bok choy, halved
4 carrots, peeled and sliced into thin matchsticks
a small bunch of fresh coriander, chopped

8 ProPoints values per serving
32 ProPoints values per recipe

343 calories per serving

Takes **25 minutes** + marinating

not recommended

1 In a bowl, mix together the ginger, garlic, oyster sauce, sweet chilli sauce and soy sauce. Place the salmon in the bowl and cover with the marinade. Refrigerate for at least 15 minutes and up to 1 hour.

2 Preheat the oven to Gas Mark 7/220°C/fan oven 200°C. Arrange the fish, skin side down, on a non stick baking tray. Pour over the marinade and bake for 15–20 minutes, basting with the marinade every 5 minutes or so, until just cooked through, golden brown and caramelised on the top.

3 Meanwhile, bring about 2.5 cm (1 inch) of water to the boil in a lidded saucepan, put the bok choy and carrots into a steamer basket and place over the boiling water. Cover and steam for about 2 minutes or until just tender – the carrots should be al dente.

4 Toss the bok choy and carrots with the coriander and arrange on four warmed plates. Drizzle with a little soy sauce, arrange the salmon on top and pour over some of the marinade from the baking tray to serve.

Tip If you can't find bok choy use pak choi instead. The **ProPoints** values will remain the same.

Chilli Beef with Noodles

A little prime fillet of beef goes a long way in this quick dish. This is a perfect meal for two.

Serves 2

1 teaspoon vegetable oil

175 g (6 oz) fillet of beef, sliced thinly

1 small onion, quartered and the layers separated

1 red pepper, de-seeded and cut into bite size pieces

100 g (3½ oz) frozen broad beans

½–1 teaspoon chilli powder or a few drops of tabasco sauce

½ teaspoon dried oregano

50 g (1¾ oz) dried tagliarini pasta or fine egg noodles

200 ml (7 fl oz) hot beef stock

1 tablespoon dry sherry

1 tablespoon light soy sauce

200 g can artichoke hearts in water, drained and sliced lengthways into 3, or canned celery hearts (optional)

9 *ProPoints* values per serving
18 *ProPoints* values per recipe

383 calories per serving

Takes **20 minutes**

not recommended

1 Heat the oil in a lidded non stick pan and stir fry the beef for 2 minutes until browned on all sides. Remove to a plate with a slotted spoon.

2 Add the onion, pepper and broad beans. Cook for 2 minutes, then stir in the chilli and oregano. Mix in the pasta or noodles, stock, sherry and soy sauce. Cover and simmer for 4–5 minutes.

3 Return the beef to the pan together with the artichoke or celery hearts and simmer for 1 minute to heat through. Serve.

Tip Canned artichokes are much easier to use than the raw version. Mild yet succulent, they are very good in tomato-based dishes, salads and pasta dishes.

Chicken Pad Thai

Pad Thai is a favourite Thai dish, and this version can be enjoyed without using up much of your daily *ProPoints* allowance.

Serves 4

125 g (4½ oz) dried rice noodles
a kettleful of boiling water
calorie controlled cooking spray
2 garlic cloves, crushed
2 cm (¾ inch) fresh root ginger, chopped finely
1 egg, beaten
300 g (10½ oz) skinless boneless chicken
   breasts, cut into strips
3 spring onions, chopped
½ teaspoon chilli flakes
2 carrots, peeled and grated
125 g (4½ oz) beansprouts
3 tablespoons soy sauce
50 g (1¾ oz) dry roasted peanuts, crushed
   roughly

7 *ProPoints* values per serving
30 *ProPoints* values per recipe

313 calories per serving

Takes **35–40 minutes**

✱ not recommended

1 Place the noodles in a large bowl and cover them with boiling water. Leave to stand for 4 minutes, then drain and refresh with cold water. Drain again and set aside.

2 Heat a wok or large non stick frying pan and spray with the cooking spray. When it is quite hot add the garlic, ginger and the egg.

3 Using chopsticks or a wooden spatula, move the egg around to scramble it until it is cooked. Remove the mixture from the pan and set aside.

4 Spray the wok or pan again with the cooking spray and add the chicken strips. Stir fry for 8–10 minutes, then add the spring onions and chilli flakes. Stir fry for another 2–3 minutes.

5 Add the noodles, carrots and all but a small handful of the beansprouts. Continue to stir fry for 3–4 minutes. Add the soy sauce, egg mixture and all but 2 tablespoons of the peanuts. Stir fry for a further 3–4 minutes.

6 Serve sprinkled with the remaining beansprouts and peanuts.

Tips Soy sauce is quite salty, so this recipe does not require any other seasoning.

For this recipe using chopsticks to cook with is much easier as it helps to separate the noodles when stir frying.

Variation For a non meat version you can omit the chicken and replace it with 250 g (9 oz) of prawns. The *ProPoints* values per serving will remain the same.

Chinese Meatballs

Serve with 60 g (2 oz) of dried brown rice per person, cooked according to packet instructions, and some zero *ProPoints* value vegetables, for an additional 6 *ProPoints* values per serving.

Serves 4

220 g can water chestnuts, drained
500 g (1 lb 2 oz) extra lean pork mince
½ tablespoon Chinese five spice
calorie controlled cooking spray
2 tablespoons cornflour
3 tablespoons dark soy sauce
1 red chilli, de-seeded and diced

6 *ProPoints* values per serving
24 *ProPoints* values per recipe

188 calories per serving

Takes **20 minutes**

* recommended

1 Chop a third of the water chestnuts finely and mix them in a bowl with the pork mince and Chinese five spice. Shape into 20 meatballs.

2 Lightly spray a non stick frying pan with the cooking spray and cook the meatballs for 12–13 minutes over a medium heat, turning to brown them evenly.

3 Meanwhile, mix the cornflour and soy sauce together in a measuring jug and then add 300 ml (10 fl oz) of cold water and the chilli.

4 Slice the remaining water chestnuts in half and add these to the frying pan, along with the soy sauce mixture. Simmer for 2 minutes until the sauce is thickened and clear. Serve immediately.

Vegetable Coconut Stir Fry

A tasty and quick vegetarian dish – perfect for entertaining at the last minute.

6 ProPoints value

Serves 4

110 g (4 oz) dried basmati rice
calorie controlled cooking spray
2 cm (¾ inch) fresh root ginger, grated
2 garlic cloves, crushed
½ teaspoon ground coriander
500 g (1 lb 2 oz) zero *ProPoints* value stir fry
vegetables (e.g. courgette, carrot, broccoli,
beansprouts, leeks and mange tout)
125 g (4½ oz) fresh baby spinach or pak choi
salt and freshly ground black pepper

To garnish

50 g (1¾ oz) shredded or desiccated coconut
a bunch of fresh coriander, chopped
2 tablespoons sesame seeds, to garnish

**6 *ProPoints* values per serving
23 *ProPoints* values per recipe**

288 calories per serving

Takes **5 minutes** to prepare,
15–20 minutes to cook

V

✱ not recommended

1 Bring a pan of water to the boil, add the rice and cook according to the packet instructions.

2 Heat a non stick wok or large frying pan, spray with the cooking spray, add the ginger, garlic and ground coriander and cook for 1–2 minutes.

3 Add the stir fry vegetables and stir fry for 12–15 minutes.

4 Stir in the spinach or pak choi and cook until it has wilted. Check the seasoning.

5 Divide the rice between four plates and top with the vegetables. Sprinkle with the coconut, coriander and sesame seeds and serve.

Variation For those that love seafood, 125 g (4½ oz) of cooked prawns could be added to this dish at the same time as the spinach or pak choi. The ***ProPoints*** values will be 7 per serving.

Sweet and Sour Pork Chops

A colourful, delicious way to brighten up pork chops. Serve with 60 g (2 oz) of dried rice per person, cooked according to packet instructions, for an additional 6 *ProPoints* values per serving.

Serves 4

4 x 150 g (5½ oz) pork loin chops, trimmed of visible fat
1 teaspoon sunflower oil
1 red pepper, de-seeded and thinly sliced
1 green pepper, deseeded and thinly sliced
1 carrot, peeled and cut into thin sticks
6 spring onions, trimmed and sliced
200 g (7 oz) canned pineapple chunks in natural juice
1 tablespoon white wine vinegar
1 tablespoon demerara sugar
2 tablespoons tomato ketchup
1 tablespoon cornflour

8 *ProPoints* values per serving
32 *ProPoints* values per recipe

365 calories per serving

Takes **15 minutes** to prepare, **20 minutes** to cook

✳ recommended

1 Preheat the grill to medium and line the grill pan with foil. Grill the chops on both sides until cooked through. This will take about 15 minutes.

2 Meanwhile, heat the oil in a non stick pan or wok and stir fry the peppers and carrot for 5 minutes. Add the spring onions and cook for a further 2 minutes.

3 Drain the pineapple, reserving the juice, and add to the pan. Mix the reserved juice with the vinegar, sugar, ketchup and cornflour. Add to the pan and cook, stirring, until the juices thicken.

4 Serve the cooked pork chops on warmed serving plates and top with the sweet and sour sauce.

Prawn Laksa

This Malaysian soup is very popular throughout Southeast Asia.

Serves 4

125 g (4½ oz) dried rice noodles
a kettleful of boiling water
calorie controlled cooking spray
4 shallots, sliced
2 teaspoons ready prepared 'fresh' lemongrass
2 teaspoons grated fresh root ginger
200 ml (7 fl oz) reduced fat coconut milk
200 ml (7 fl oz) vegetable stock
3–4 teaspoons Thai red curry paste
1 tablespoon Thai fish sauce or light soy sauce
450 g (1 lb) large peeled prawns, defrosted if frozen
1 tablespoon chopped fresh coriander, plus extra to garnish
finely sliced red chillies, to garnish

8 ProPoints values per serving
32 ProPoints values per recipe

315 calories per serving

Takes **30 minutes**

✳ not recommended

1 Put the rice noodles into a bowl, cover with boiling water and soak for 4 minutes.

2 Meanwhile, lightly spray a non stick wok or large frying pan with the cooking spray and sauté the shallots for about 3 minutes, until softened. Add the lemongrass, ginger, coconut milk, stock, curry paste and fish or soy sauce. Heat until almost boiling.

3 Add the prawns to the wok or frying pan with the chopped coriander and cook gently for 2 minutes. Add the drained noodles and cook for a further 2 minutes, until they are heated through.

4 Serve the laksa in four warmed bowls, garnished with the sliced chillies and coriander.

Chicken and Mango Stir Fry

Stir frying a colourful mix of vegetables always looks attractive and, what's more, it tastes great. Serve with 40 g (1½ oz) of dried noodles per person, cooked according to packet instructions, for an additional 4 *ProPoints* values per serving.

Serves 2

calorie controlled cooking spray

225 g (8 oz) skinless boneless chicken breasts, cut into strips

1 garlic clove, crushed

1 red chilli, de-seeded and chopped finely

2.5 cm (1 inch) fresh root ginger, grated

175 g (6 oz) broccoli, broken into florets

125 g (4½ oz) mange tout

125 g (4½ oz) baby sweetcorn, halved

100 g (3½ oz) canned bamboo shoots, drained

225 g (8 oz) mango, peeled and cubed

4 tablespoons ginger wine

2 tablespoons tomato purée

2 tablespoons soy sauce

1 teaspoon cornflour

---

4 *ProPoints* values per serving
9 *ProPoints* values per recipe

311 **calories** per serving

Takes **30 minutes**

recommended

1 Heat a large non stick frying pan or wok and spray it with the cooking spray. Add the chicken strips and stir fry for 5 minutes until the chicken has browned evenly.

2 Add the garlic, chilli, ginger, broccoli, mange tout and baby sweetcorn and stir fry for a further 5 minutes.

3 Add the bamboo shoots and mango and heat through for 2 minutes.

4 Mix together the ginger wine, tomato purée, soy sauce and cornflour and add this to the pan. Cook, stirring, until the sauce thickens. Spoon on to warmed plates and serve.

Variation For a vegetarian version, use 225 g (8 oz) of finely diced tofu instead of the chicken, for 5 *ProPoints* values per serving.

Tofu with Green Thai Curry Sauce

Cooking tofu gently in the curry sauce allows it to absorb all the delicious flavours.

Serves 2

2 tablespoons green Thai curry paste
125 g (4½ oz) tofu, cubed
200 ml (7 fl oz) reduced fat coconut milk
200 ml (7 fl oz) vegetable stock
200 g (7 oz) sweet potatoes, peeled and cubed
75 g (2¾ oz) sugarsnap peas
1 small red pepper, de-seeded and sliced
a handful of sliced spring onions, to garnish

8 **ProPoints** values per serving
16 **ProPoints** values per recipe

C 331 calories per serving

Takes **15 minutes** to prepare,
20 minutes to cook

V

✱ not recommended

1 Heat a lidded non stick saucepan until hot. Put the paste and the tofu in the saucepan and stir fry for 1–2 minutes.

2 Add the coconut milk, stock and sweet potatoes. Bring to the boil, cover and simmer for 15 minutes until the potatoes are just tender.

3 Add the sugarsnap peas and pepper. Cook for a further 5 minutes.

4 Serve garnished with the spring onions.

Tip For an extra treat, serve with coconut rice. For 2 people, cook 110 g (4 oz) of dried Thai or long grain rice according to the packet instructions. Meanwhile, dry fry 1 tablespoon of desiccated coconut, then toss into the rice before serving. This will be an additional 6 **ProPoints** values per serving.

Baked Chinese Trout

This tastes even better with some fennel seeds sprinkled inside the fish just before it is baked.

Serve with 40 g (1½ oz) of dried noodles, cooked according to packet instructions, for an additional 4 *ProPoints* values.

Serves 1

½ teaspoon sesame oil
2 teaspoons dark soy sauce
½ teaspoon Chinese five spice
250 g (9 oz) trout, gutted and scaled and, if desired, head removed
salt and freshly ground black pepper

7 *ProPoints* values per serving
7 *ProPoints* values per recipe

297 calories per serving

Takes **5 minutes** to prepare,
25 minutes to cook

✳ not recommended

1 Preheat the oven to Gas Mark 6/200°C/fan oven 180°C. Combine the oil, soy sauce and Chinese five spice and coat the fish. Season to taste.

2 Place the fish on a non stick baking tray and roast for 25 minutes, until the skin is crisp. Serve immediately.

Chilli Fried Rice with Prawns

A spicy rice dish that is perfect for a light supper.

Serves 4

225 g (8 oz) dried long grain rice
2 tablespoons vegetable oil
2 garlic cloves, finely chopped
1 small red chilli, de-seeded and finely chopped
8 shallots, finely sliced
1 tablespoon Thai red curry paste
1 red pepper, de-seeded and chopped
100 g (3½ oz) fine green beans, chopped
225 g (8 oz) raw peeled prawns, defrosted
   if frozen
2 tablespoons Thai fish sauce or light soy sauce,
   to taste
salt and freshly ground black pepper

To serve
cucumber, chopped
spring onions, chopped
fresh red or green chilli, de-seeded and thinly
   sliced

9 ProPoints values per serving
36 ProPoints values per recipe

369 calories per serving

Takes **15 minutes** to prepare,
15 minutes to cook

✷ Freezing recommended (before adding prawns)

1 Bring a pan of water to the boil, add the rice and cook according to the packet instructions until tender. Rinse with cold water and drain thoroughly.

2 Meanwhile, heat the oil in a non stick wok or large non stick frying pan and add the garlic. Cook gently for 2 minutes until golden. Add the chilli and shallots and cook, stirring, for another 3–4 minutes.

3 Stir in the Thai curry paste and cook gently for 1 minute, then add the red pepper and green beans. Stir fry briskly for 2 minutes.

4 Tip the cooked rice into the wok or frying pan and add the prawns. Stir fry over a medium-high heat for about 4–5 minutes, until the rice is piping hot and the prawns have turned pink.

5 Season to taste with the fish sauce or soy sauce and seasoning, if necessary. Pile on to warmed serving plates and garnish with the cucumber, spring onions and fresh chilli.

Tip You can use cooked peeled prawns if you prefer, though they will not need to be cooked for long. Add them when the rice has been reheated and just cook them for about 2 minutes, or else they will toughen.

Burmese-style Lamb Steaks

This will awaken your taste buds, as it is sweet, sour and hot. Serve with 100 g (3½ oz) of boiled potatoes and asparagus per person, for an additional 2 *ProPoints* values per serving.

Serves 4

4 x 100 g (3½ oz) lean lamb leg steaks, trimmed of visible fat
½ tablespoon plain flour
1 small onion, chopped finely
1 red chilli, de-seeded and chopped finely
1 tablespoon medium curry paste
1 teaspoon lemongrass purée
calorie controlled cooking spray
1 teaspoon tamarind paste
2 tablespoons boiling water
5 g (¼ oz) anchovies in salt, rinsed and chopped finely
250 ml (9 fl oz) hot vegetable stock
2 teaspoons soft brown sugar

7 *ProPoints* values per serving
27 *ProPoints* values per recipe

266 calories per serving

Takes **23 minutes**

✳ recommended (sauce only)

1 Put the lamb steaks in a bowl and dust with the plain flour. Add the onion, chilli, curry paste and lemongrass purée. Mix to coat.

2 Heat a wide non stick saucepan and spray with the cooking spray. Cook the steaks for 2 minutes on each side until brown.

3 Mix the tamarind paste with the boiling water and stir in the anchovies, stock and sugar. Bring back to the boil.

4 Lower the heat and simmer for 10 minutes until thickened. Serve immediately.

Thai Green Pumpkin Curry

This recipe follows the authentic Thai method for making curries. The stock, paste and coconut milk are boiled first, and the other ingredients are then added. This means you don't need to add oil, making a delicious yet low **ProPoints** values curry.

Serves 4

600 ml (20 fl oz) vegetable stock
2 tablespoons Thai green curry paste
25 g (1 oz) creamed coconut, crumbled
6 shallots, halved
2 garlic cloves, sliced thinly
450 g (1 lb) pumpkin or butternut squash, peeled, de-seeded and cubed
150 g (5½ oz) fine green beans, sliced
225 g (8 oz) cherry tomatoes, halved
3 tablespoons chopped fresh coriander, to serve

2 ProPoints values per serving
7 ProPoints values per recipe

108 calories per serving

Takes **25 minutes** to prepare,
25 minutes to cook

V

✴ recommended

1 Pour the stock into a large saucepan and add the curry paste and creamed coconut. Bring to the boil, stirring, until the coconut dissolves.

2 Boil the sauce rapidly for 5 minutes, then add the shallots, garlic, pumpkin or butternut squash and green beans. Cook over a medium heat, so it keeps bubbling, for 20 minutes or until the pumpkin or squash is tender.

3 Add the tomatoes and cook for a further 5 minutes. Sprinkle over the coriander just before serving.

Tip The consistency of Thai curries is generally quite soup-like and they are often served with jasmine rice, which has a sticky texture; this helps to soak up the wonderful sauce. Serve with 60 g (2 oz) of dried jasmine rice per person, cooked according to packet instructions, for an additional 6 **ProPoints** values per serving.

Chinese Five Spice Chicken

Chinese five spice contains aniseed, cinnamon, fennel, black pepper and cloves and imparts a very distinctive Chinese aroma and warm flavour to chicken. Serve with 40 g (1½ oz) of dried egg noodles per person, cooked according to packet instructions, for an additional 4 *ProPoints* values per serving.

Serves 4

600 g (1 lb 5 oz) skinless boneless chicken breasts, cut into bite size pieces

450 g (1 lb) carrots, peeled and sliced thinly on the diagonal

300 ml (10 fl oz) chicken stock

1 tablespoon cornflour

a bunch of spring onions, sliced finely on the diagonal

For the marinade

1 tablespoon Chinese five spice

1 tablespoon honey

2 tablespoons soy sauce

1 tablespoon rice vinegar

1 teaspoon sesame oil

2.5 cm (1 inch) fresh root ginger, grated

6 *ProPoints* values per serving
24 *ProPoints* values per recipe

280 calories per serving

Takes **10 minutes** to prepare +
30 minutes–12 hours marinating,
15 minutes to cook

✱ not recommended

1 Place all the marinade ingredients in a small pan and heat gently, stirring. Place the chicken in a shallow bowl or tray and pour the marinade over. Cover with cling film and leave in the refrigerator for a minimum of 30 minutes, preferably overnight.

2 Heat a large non stick frying pan or wok, add the chicken, marinade and carrots and stir fry over a high heat for 5 minutes. Add the stock, bring to the boil and boil rapidly for 5 minutes.

3 Mix the cornflour to a paste with 1 tablespoon of water. Stir into the frying pan or wok with the spring onions.

4 Bring the sauce back to the boil, stirring until it becomes thick and glossy, then serve.

Steamed Mussels with Lemongrass

A delicious and different way to cook mussels. Serve as a light lunch or supper dish.

Serves 2

2 teaspoons vegetable oil
1 onion, chopped
4 garlic cloves, chopped
2 lemongrass stems, chopped
**1 small red chilli, de-seeded and chopped
(optional)**
300 ml (10 fl oz) vegetable stock
1 tablespoon soy sauce
100 ml (3½ fl oz) dry white wine
2 kg (4 lb 8 oz) fresh mussels, cleaned
**a small bunch of fresh basil or coriander, chopped
roughly**

10 *ProPoints* values per serving
20 *ProPoints* values per recipe

426 calories per serving

Takes **35 minutes**

✳ not recommended

1 Heat the oil in a large, lidded, non stick saucepan, then add the onion, garlic and lemongrass. Fry gently for a few minutes, then add the chilli, if using, stock, soy sauce and white wine.

2 Add the mussels, discarding any that are open or broken, cover with a lid and cook for 3–4 minutes, shaking occasionally, or until the mussels open (do not overcook or they will become tough).

3 Discard any mussels that have not opened. Add the basil or coriander, toss together and then ladle the mussels and all the juices into bowls or soup plates.

Tips To prepare mussels, discard any open ones then scrub the shells with a brush. Remove and discard the beards and then soak the mussels in a sinkful of cold water for at least 10 minutes, before draining and rinsing, then draining again.

You can serve this as a starter for 4 people, for 5 *ProPoints* values per serving.

Thai-style Chilli Beef

7 ProPoints value

This delicious Thai style meal is full of flavour and makes for a spicy end to the day.

Serves 4

400 g (14 oz) beef fillet steak, sliced thinly
2 garlic cloves, crushed
4 tablespoons Thai fish sauce
1 tablespoon dark soy sauce
2 tablespoons oyster sauce
2–3 teaspoons chilli paste with no added oil
  (see Tip)
2 teaspoons caster sugar
2 tablespoons fresh coriander, chopped
2 lemongrass stems, chopped finely
100 g (3½ oz) dried thick rice noodles
a kettleful of boiling water
calorie controlled cooking spray
a large bunch of spring onions, chopped
150 g (5½ oz) sugarsnap peas, halved
  lengthways
4 leaves from a Chinese leaf lettuce, shredded
200 g (7 oz) beansprouts
½ red pepper, de-seeded and sliced
4 tomatoes, quartered
salt and freshly ground black pepper

7 ProPoints values per serving
27 ProPoints values per recipe

313 calories per serving

Takes **10 minutes** to prepare,
15 minutes to cook + marinating

✳ not recommended

1 Mix the beef, garlic, sauces, chilli paste, sugar, coriander and lemongrass together in a lidded dish or non metallic bowl. Cover and marinate in a fridge for several hours or overnight.

2 Place the noodles in a heatproof bowl, cover with boiling water and leave for 5 minutes then drain, or prepare according to the packet instructions.

3 Meanwhile, spray a large non stick wok or frying pan with the cooking spray and stir fry the beef and marinade for two minutes or until the beef is browned. Remove and put to one side.

4 Add the spring onions to the wok or frying pan and fry for a minute or so, then add the remaining vegetables. Stir fry for a further 5 minutes or until the vegetables are tender but still slightly crunchy.

5 Refresh the noodles by rinsing with cold water, drain thoroughly and add them to the wok, together with the beef. Heat through and serve immediately.

Tips The problem with chillies is that you don't really know how hot they are until you've put them in your food. You can find pastes in tubes and jars made just from chillies with no added oil. These have a *ProPoints* value of zero. Once you know how much you like, your recipe will be the same strength every time.

If you want to use fresh chillies, use 1–2 depending on how hot you like your food and how strong the chillies are.

Red Pork Curry

Kafir lime leaves add an authentic flavour to this Thai curry.

Serves 4

calorie controlled cooking spray
**500 g (1 lb 2 oz) lean pork tenderloin, cut into
  even chunks**
4 shallots, sliced
1 teaspoon ginger purée
1½ tablespoons red Thai curry paste
150 g (5½ oz) low fat soft cheese
4 dried kaffir lime leaves
500 ml (18 fl oz) hot vegetable stock
**100 g (3½ oz) fine green beans, trimmed and
  halved**
40 g (1½ oz) desiccated coconut
salt and freshly ground black pepper

8 ProPoints values per serving
32 ProPoints values per recipe

313 calories per serving

Takes **25 minutes**

recommended

1 Heat a wide, lidded, non stick saucepan and spray with the cooking spray. Cook the pork for 5 minutes, stirring until browned all over. Add the shallots, ginger purée and curry paste and cook gently for 3 minutes.

2 Stir in the soft cheese and lime leaves and gradually add the stock. Bring to a simmer and cook for 5 minutes.

3 Add the beans and coconut. Cover and simmer for a further 5 minutes until the pork is cooked and the sauce has thickened. Season to taste and serve immediately.

Variation For a vegetarian version, replace the pork with a 350 g packet of Quorn pieces, for a **ProPoints** value of 6 per serving.

Quick Thai Chicken Curry with Rice Noodles

This Thai-style chicken curry is made in no time and it's full of wonderful flavours.

Serves 4

1 tablespoon stir fry oil or vegetable oil
a bunch of spring onions, chopped
350 g (12 oz) skinless boneless chicken breasts, cut into large chunks
1 cm (½ inch) fresh root ginger, finely grated
finely grated zest of a lime or lemon
100 ml (3½ fl oz) reduced fat coconut milk
125 ml (4 fl oz) chicken stock
2 tablespoons Thai red or green curry paste
1 tablespoon light soy sauce
1 tablespoon chopped fresh basil or coriander
175 g (6 oz) dried rice noodles
salt and freshly ground black pepper

To garnish
chopped spring onions
lime slices
basil or coriander sprigs

10 ProPoints values per serving
38 ProPoints values per recipe

367 calories per serving

Takes **15 minutes** to prepare,
25 minutes to cook

✳ recommended (without the noodles)

1 Heat the oil in a large, lidded, non stick frying pan and sauté the spring onions until softened, about 2 minutes. Add the chicken and cook for 3 more minutes, until sealed on the outside.

2 Add the ginger, lime or lemon zest, coconut milk, stock, curry paste, soy sauce and basil or coriander. Heat until almost boiling. Cover and simmer gently over a low heat for 15–20 minutes, until the chicken is cooked.

3 Meanwhile, bring a pan of water to the boil, add the rice noodles and cook for about 6 minutes, or according to packet instructions, then drain.

4 Season the chicken curry and garnish with the chopped spring onions, lime slices and sprigs of fresh basil or coriander. Serve with the cooked noodles.

Tip Look out for Thai red or green curry paste, coconut milk and rice noodles in the Oriental foods section of your supermarket, or ask for them at your local delicatessen.

Star Anise Beef Stew

Here is an Asian idea of a stew – more of a fragrant soup with tender morsels of beef.

Serves 4

1 litre (1¾ pints) vegetable or chicken stock
450 g (1 lb) beef steak, cut into thin slivers
3 garlic cloves, chopped finely
2 cinnamon sticks
4 star anise
3 tablespoons soy sauce
1 teaspoon artificial sweetener
125 g (4½ oz) beansprouts

To garnish

1 spring onion, chopped finely
a small bunch of fresh coriander, chopped
  roughly

6 *ProPoints* values per serving
25 *ProPoints* values per recipe

261 calories per serving

Takes **15 minutes** to prepare,
30 minutes to cook

✳ not recommended

1 Put the stock in a large saucepan with the beef, garlic, cinnamon, star anise, soy sauce and sweetener. Bring to the boil and simmer for 30 minutes, occasionally skimming any scum off the top.

2 Meanwhile, put the beansprouts into the bottom of four serving bowls. Ladle the hot soup over the beansprouts and garnish with the spring onion and coriander.

Sweet and Sour Prawns

This recipe is so fast, it's quicker than going to get a takeaway.

Serves 4

1 tablespoon cornflour
300 ml (10 fl oz) pineapple juice
1 tablespoon light soy sauce
1 tablespoon tomato purée
2 tablespoons rice vinegar or wine vinegar
calorie controlled cooking spray
1 red pepper, de-seeded and sliced
1 green pepper, de-seeded and sliced
a bunch of spring onions, halved and then split
  in 2 lengthways
200 g (7 oz) sugarsnap peas, halved lengthways
100 g (3½ oz) baby sweetcorn, halved
  lengthways
227 g tin water chestnuts, drained and halved
240 g (8½ oz) dried fine egg noodles
200 g (7 oz) beansprouts
250 g (9 oz) cooked and peeled prawns,
  defrosted if frozen
salt and freshly ground black pepper

9 *ProPoints* values per serving
35 *ProPoints* values per recipe

403 calories per serving

Takes **10 minutes**

not recommended

1 In a jug, mix the cornflour with a little of the pineapple juice to make a smooth paste. Add the remaining juice, soy sauce, tomato purée and rice or wine vinegar and mix thoroughly. Transfer to a small saucepan and heat gently, stirring occasionally until thickened.

2 Meanwhile, spray a large non stick wok or non stick frying pan with the cooking spray and place it over a high heat. Add the peppers and spring onions and stir fry for a couple of minutes.

3 Add the sugarsnap peas and fry for a further 3 minutes, then add the sweetcorn and water chestnuts. Pour the hot sauce into the wok or frying pan, combine well and cook for 2–3 minutes.

4 Meanwhile, bring a large pan of water to the boil and add the noodles. Bring back to the boil and simmer for 3 minutes, then drain.

5 Add the beansprouts and prawns to the wok or frying pan and cook for a final 2–3 minutes, or until the prawns are very hot and the beansprouts are tender. Check the seasoning and serve immediately with the noodles.

Variation You can substitute 60 g (2 oz) of dried rice per person, cooked according to packet instructions, for the noodles, for 8 ***ProPoints*** values per serving.

Suppers with Spice

Spice isn't just for curries; liven up an everyday supper with something special that everyone will love. Try Spicy Turkey Marrow, Prawn and Saffron Gumbo, Caribbean Roast Pork or Chilli Beef Tacos.

Spicy recipes for everyday or
for a special meal

North African Stuffed Plaice

10 ProPoints value

This quick and tasty stuffed plaice is full of wonderful flavours of herbs and spices.

Serves 2

1 small onion, chopped finely
2 carrots, peeled and grated
a small bunch of fresh mint, chopped
1 teaspoon chilli sauce
1 garlic clove, crushed
1 teaspoon ground turmeric
½ teaspoon dried ginger
2 tablespoons low fat natural yogurt
2 x 130 g (4½ oz) plaice fillets
400 g can chopped tomatoes
125 g (4½ oz) dried couscous
300 ml (10 fl oz) hot vegetable stock
salt and freshly ground black pepper

---

10 ProPoints values per serving
20 ProPoints values per recipe

C **449 calories** per serving

Takes **10 minutes** to prepare,
30 minutes to cook

* not recommended

1 Preheat the oven to Gas Mark 4/180°C/fan oven 160°C. In a large bowl, mix together the onion, carrots, mint, chilli sauce, garlic, spices and yogurt to make the stuffing.

2 Place a large piece of kitchen foil on a baking tray – large enough to fold over the fish to make a parcel – and lay the plaice fillets in the middle. Spoon the stuffing over each fish and carefully fold over the fillets to encase the filling.

3 Pour the tomatoes over the fish. Season and make a loose parcel with the foil, scrunching and folding the edges so that the fish is sealed in. Bake in the oven for 30 minutes.

4 About 5 minutes before the fish is ready, place the couscous in a bowl and pour over the stock – make sure it is boiling hot. Cover and leave for 5 minutes, then fluff up with a fork. Serve the couscous with the fish and spoon over the juices from inside the foil parcel.

Tip Use a teaspoon of mint sauce if you cannot find fresh mint.

Variation Try using the same amount of courgettes instead of carrots, and fresh coriander instead of mint. The **ProPoints** values will remain the same.

Chicken Tagine with Lemon Couscous

Serves 2

calorie controlled cooking spray

2 x 125 g (4½ oz) skinless boneless chicken breasts

1 red pepper, de-seeded and sliced

1 onion, chopped

2 garlic cloves, crushed

1 teaspoon ground cinnamon

1 teaspoon ground cumin

½ teaspoon turmeric

2 tomatoes, chopped

250 ml (9 fl oz) chicken stock

411 g can apricots in natural juice, drained and sliced

2 tablespoons chopped fresh coriander, to garnish

For the couscous

125 g (4½ oz) couscous

150 ml (5 fl oz) hot chicken stock

75 g (2¾ oz) steamed green beans, chopped into 5 cm (2 inch) pieces

grated zest and juice of ½ a lemon

salt and freshly ground black pepper

⟮ **10 ProPoints** values per serving
20 ProPoints values per recipe

C **530 calories** per serving

⊙ Takes **30 minutes** to prepare +
10 minutes soaking, **20 minutes** to cook

✱ recommended (stew only)

1 Spray a lidded non stick frying pan with the cooking spray and heat until hot. Add the chicken breasts and cook for 3 minutes, turning once, until browned on both sides. Remove from the pan.

2 Spray the pan again with the cooking spray and add the pepper and onion. Stir fry for 5 minutes until just tender. Add the garlic and spices and continue cooking for 1 minute. Return the chicken to the pan with the tomatoes and stock. Cover and simmer over a low heat for 15 minutes. Add the apricots and cook for another 5 minutes until the chicken is tender.

3 Meanwhile, to prepare the couscous, place it in a bowl, pour over the hot stock and cover with cling film. Set aside to soak for 10 minutes. Fluff with a fork, stir in the beans and lemon zest and juice, then season.

4 Serve the chicken tagine with a pile of the couscous and the coriander sprinkled over.

Tip If you like spicy food, add 1 teaspoon of hot chilli powder with the spices in step 2, for no additional **ProPoints** values.

Spicy Sausage and Butter Bean Casserole

Sausages and beans – a perfect hot dish for Bonfire Night.

Serves 4

450 g (1 lb) low fat pork sausages
400 g can chopped tomatoes
2 tablespoons tomato purée
300 ml (10 fl oz) pork stock
1 tablespoon Worcestershire sauce
225 g (8 oz) button mushrooms, halved
225 g (8 oz) baby onions, halved
1 green pepper, de-seeded and sliced
1 teaspoon chilli sauce
410 g can butter beans, drained and rinsed
salt and freshly ground black pepper
1 tablespoon chopped fresh flat leaf parsley, to garnish

9 ProPoints values per serving
35 ProPoints values per recipe

C **367 calories** per serving

Takes **20 minutes** to prepare, **35 minutes** to cook

✱ recommended

1 Preheat the grill to medium and line the grill pan with foil. Grill the sausages for 10 minutes, turning frequently, until they are evenly browned.

2 Meanwhile, place the tomatoes, tomato purée, stock and Worcestershire sauce in a flameproof casserole dish and bring to the boil. Stir in the mushrooms, onions, pepper and chilli sauce and simmer for 10 minutes.

3 Add the grilled sausages and butter beans to the sauce and season to taste. Simmer for a further 20 minutes. Sprinkle with the parsley and serve.

Tip Although it's not essential to grill the sausages, a good colour enhances the look of the finished dish.

Spicy Swede Ratatouille

Serve as a side dish or with 60 g (2 oz) of dried rice per person, cooked according to packet instructions, for an additional 6 **ProPoints** values per serving.

Serves 4

1 swede, peeled and cut into chunks
500 g (1 lb 2 oz) passata
1 onion, chopped
500 g (1 lb 2 oz) mushrooms, sliced
2 courgettes, sliced
2 garlic cloves, crushed
1 small red chilli, de-seeded and chopped finely
2 teaspoons grated fresh root ginger
salt and freshly ground black pepper

0 ProPoints values per serving
0 ProPoints values per recipe

91 calories per serving

Takes **15 minutes** to prepare,
1½ hours to cook

V

✳ recommended

1 Preheat the oven to Gas Mark 4/180°C/fan oven 160°C. Bring a pan of water to the boil, add the swede and cook for about 10 minutes, until almost tender. Drain well.

2 Put the swede into a large, lidded, ovenproof casserole dish with the passata. Add all the other ingredients, stir together and season.

3 Cover and cook in the oven for 1¼–1½ hours.

Variation Use 200 g (7 oz) of potatoes instead of the swede, for 1 **ProPoints** value per serving.

Vegetable Enchiladas

Mexican style soft tortillas are used in this easy recipe. They are available from most supermarkets and delicatessens, so do try them in this excellent vegetarian dish.

Serves 4

calorie controlled cooking spray
1 onion, chopped
1–2 garlic cloves, crushed
1 red pepper, de-seeded and chopped
1 small aubergine, chopped
100 g (3½ oz) mushrooms, sliced
400 g can chick peas, drained and rinsed
1 teaspoon mild chilli powder
2 tablespoons tomato purée
2 tablespoons chopped fresh coriander
4 soft flour tortillas
100 g (3½ oz) half fat Cheddar cheese, grated
salt and freshly ground black pepper
sprigs of fresh coriander, to garnish (optional)

7 **ProPoints** values per serving
30 **ProPoints** values per recipe

C 313 calories per serving

Takes **20 minutes** to prepare,
20–25 minutes to cook

V

✳ recommended before baking

1 Preheat the oven to Gas Mark 4/180°C/fan oven 160°C. Spray a 1.5 litre (2¾ pint) ovenproof baking dish with the cooking spray.

2 Heat a large non stick frying pan and spray it with the cooking spray. Add the onion, garlic, pepper, aubergine and mushrooms and sauté them for about 5 minutes, until softened.

3 Add the chick peas and chilli powder to the pan. Cook for about 5 minutes, stirring often. Stir in the tomato purée and coriander. Season and remove from the heat.

4 Lay the tortillas on a work surface and divide the filling equally between them. Roll them up and place them in the baking dish. Scatter the grated cheese on top and bake in the oven for 20–25 minutes.

5 Serve the tortillas, garnished with the sprigs of fresh coriander, if using.

Tip Why not serve a zero **ProPoints** value home made salsa with the enchiladas? Just mix together finely chopped red onion, cucumber, tomatoes and fresh coriander or parsley. Flavour it with lime juice, chilli sauce and seasoning.

Variation Instead of the chick peas, use 175 g (6 oz) of canned or frozen sweetcorn. The **ProPoints** values per serving will be the same.

Tangy Lamb Souvlaki

Serve these sweet and spicy lamb skewers with a generous zero *ProPoints* value mixed salad.

Serves 4

8 long, tough fresh rosemary sprigs (for skewers)

250 g (9 oz) fresh apricots, stoned and chopped roughly

2 tablespoons white wine vinegar

2 garlic cloves

1 tablespoon artificial sweetener

½ teaspoon ground allspice

4 x 125 g (4½ oz) lean lamb leg steaks, cut into bite size chunks

235 g (8½ oz) dried brown rice

12 *ProPoints* values per serving
49 *ProPoints* values per recipe

C **478 calories** per serving

Takes **50 minutes** + **30 minutes** marinating

＊ not recommended

1 To make the skewers, starting about 2.5 cm (1 inch) down from the top of each rosemary sprig, remove the leaves from the main stalk. Reserve the stalks and 1 tablespoon of the removed leaves. Discard the remaining leaves. (You can also use wooden skewers instead of rosemary skewers).

2 Put the reserved rosemary leaves into a small lidded pan along with the apricots, vinegar, garlic, sweetener, allspice and 100 ml (3½ fl oz) of water. Bring to the boil, cover and simmer for 5–10 minutes until stewed. Leave to cool for 20 minutes.

3 Meanwhile, thread the chunks of lamb on to the stripped rosemary skewers, leaving the rosemary leaves exposed at the top (or thread on to wooden skewers). Put into a shallow non metallic dish.

4 When the stewed apricots are cool, whizz in a food processor or with a hand blender until puréed. Pour half over the lamb skewers and leave for 30 minutes.

5 Meanwhile, bring a pan of water to the boil, add the rice and cook according to packet instructions. Preheat the grill to medium-high or prepare your barbecue.

6 Grill or barbecue the lamb skewers for 10–15 minutes, basting with the marinade until cooked and starting to caramelise. Transfer the skewers to plates with the rice and the reserved glaze as a chutney on the side.

Tip If using wooden skewers, soak them in water for 30 minutes first to prevent them from burning.

Bobotie

Serve this traditional South African dish with a zero *ProPoints* value mixed salad.

Serves 4

calorie controlled cooking spray
1 large onion, chopped finely
1 cooking apple, peeled, cored and chopped
500 g (1lb 2 oz) turkey mince
2 medium slices bread, broken into small pieces
2 tablespoons skimmed milk
1 tablespoon brown sugar
1 tablespoon wine vinegar
1 tablespoon tomato purée
1 tablespoon curry powder
50 g (1¾ oz) raisins
½ teaspoon salt
1 egg, beaten
juice of a lemon
6 bay leaves
salt and freshly ground black pepper

For the topping
150 g (5½ oz) low fat natural yogurt
1 egg
1 teaspoon turmeric

1 Preheat the oven to Gas Mark 4/180°C/fan oven 160°C. Spray a large non stick frying pan or wok with the cooking spray and fry the onion and apple for 5 minutes until softened. Add 1 or 2 tablespoons of water if necessary to stop them sticking.

2 Add the mince to the pan, season and cook until browned. Add the bread, milk, sugar, vinegar, tomato purée, curry powder, raisins, salt, egg and lemon juice and mix together.

3 Place the mixture in an lidded ovenproof dish and add the bay leaves. Cover and cook in the oven for 30 minutes.

4 Meanwhile, mix the topping ingredients together in a measuring jug. Make the mixture up to 250 ml (9 fl oz) with water.

5 Remove the dish from the oven, uncover and pour over the topping. Return it, uncovered, to the oven for a further 10 minutes or until the topping has set.

9 *ProPoints* values per serving
35 *ProPoints* values per recipe

379 calories per serving

Takes **15 minutes** to prepare, **40 minutes** to cook

✳ recommended (see Tip)

Tip Freeze this dish without the topping. When you are ready to eat it, heat through and then add the topping as in steps 4 and 5.

Variation Extra lean beef or lamb mince could be used instead of the turkey mince, but the *ProPoints* values per serving would increase to 10 and 12 respectively.

Pork Chops with Chilli Apples

Serves 4

1 Bramley apple, peeled, cored and chopped

2 tablespoons cider vinegar

calorie controlled cooking spray

4 x 150 g (5½ oz) lean pork loin steaks

1 onion, chopped finely

1 red chilli, de-seeded and chopped finely

150 g (5½ oz) button mushrooms, wiped and halved

300 ml (10 fl oz) vegetable stock

1 eating apple, cored and sliced thinly

2 tablespoons low fat soft cheese

1 tablespoon vegetable gravy granules

salt and freshly ground black pepper

fresh thyme sprigs, to garnish

1 To make the apple sauce, put the Bramley apple into a small lidded saucepan with the vinegar. Cover and cook gently for 5 minutes until soft and stewed. Purée with a hand held blender and set aside.

2 Heat a wide non stick frying pan and spray with the cooking spray. Brown the pork steaks on each side for 2 minutes. Remove and set aside. Add the onion, chilli and mushrooms to the pan and gently cook for 3–4 minutes until softened. Add the vegetable stock, apple slices, soft cheese and apple purée. Bring to the boil and stir in the gravy granules until thickened.

4 Return the pork steaks to the pan and simmer for 10 minutes until cooked. Season and scatter over the thyme.

8 ProPoints values per serving
31 ProPoints values per recipe

C **358 calories** per serving

Takes **30 minutes**

* not recommended

Chilli Beef Tacos

These 'fill your own' tacos make great family food, to be eaten with the hands – messy but a lot of fun.

Serves 4

For the chilli
calorie controlled cooking spray
350 g (12 oz) extra lean beef mince
1 large onion, chopped
1 red pepper, deseeded and diced
1 green pepper, deseeded and diced
2 garlic cloves, crushed
¼ teaspoon hot chilli powder
1 teaspoon ground cumin
400 g can chopped tomatoes
200 g can kidney beans, drained and rinsed
200 ml (7 fl oz) beef stock

To serve
8 taco shells
½ Iceberg lettuce, shredded
75 g (2¾ oz) half fat mature Cheddar cheese, grated

---

10 ProPoints values per serving
40 ProPoints values per recipe

424 calories per serving

Takes **20 minutes** to prepare, **30 minutes** to cook

✱ recommended (for chilli only)

1 Heat a large, lidded, non stick pan, spray with the cooking spray and brown the mince in two batches, removing to a plate when done.

2 Spray the pan again with the cooking spray, then fry the onion, peppers and garlic for 5 minutes. Add the mince and remaining chilli ingredients to the pan. Bring to a simmer, cover and cook gently for 30 minutes.

3 Warm the taco shells for 1 minute on full power in the microwave or for 3 minutes in an oven preheated to Gas Mark 4/180°C/fan oven 160°C. Put some lettuce in each taco, top with the chilli and cheese and serve.

Variations For a vegetarian version, substitute Quorn mince for the beef mince and use vegetable stock. The **ProPoints** values will be 8 per serving.

Spicy Turkey Marrow

This dish is stuffed with a tasty turkey mixture, which makes it filling and perfect for a lunch or supper dish.

Serves 4

1 marrow, halved lengthways and de-seeded
2 teaspoons vegetable oil
1 onion, chopped
1 carrot, peeled and grated
1 red pepper, de-seeded and chopped
2 garlic cloves, crushed
1 tablespoon mild curry powder or mixed spice
275 g (9½ oz) turkey mince
2 tablespoons chopped fresh mixed herbs
  (or 1 tablespoon dried)
1 tablespoon soy sauce
150 ml (5 fl oz) hot chicken stock
2 tablespoons half fat crème fraîche
salt and freshly ground black pepper

4 ProPoints values per serving
17 ProPoints values per recipe

C **198 calories** per serving

Takes **25 minutes** to prepare,
30–35 minutes to cook

✳ not recommended

1 Preheat the oven to Gas Mark 6/200°C/fan oven 180°C. Place the marrow in a large baking dish or roasting tin, cut sides up.

2 Heat the vegetable oil in a large non stick saucepan, add the onion and sauté gently for 2–3 minutes. Add the carrot, pepper and garlic and cook gently for another 3–4 minutes, until softened. Stir in the curry powder or mixed spice and cook for a further minute.

3 Stir the turkey mince into the vegetables and add the herbs and soy sauce. Cook for 2–3 minutes over a medium-high heat, then add the chicken stock. Heat until boiling, then reduce the heat and simmer for about 10 minutes until the stock has been reduced by half. Season to taste, remove from the heat and stir in the crème fraîche.

4 Spoon the turkey mixture into the hollowed out marrow halves. Add about 150 ml (5 fl oz) of cold water to the baking dish or tin (around the marrow), then cover with foil and bake for 30–35 minutes, until the marrow is tender.

Tip If you enjoy spicy food, add a little more curry powder and a generous dash of Tabasco sauce to the turkey mixture, for no extra **ProPoints** values.

Variation For a vegetarian meal, replace the turkey with a good selection of zero **ProPoints** value vegetables such as mushrooms, aubergine, celery, asparagus, mange tout and green beans and use vegetable stock instead of chicken. The **ProPoints** values per serving will be reduced to 2.

Spicy Pizza

A great recipe for all your friends to enjoy.

9 ProPoints value

Serves 4

200 g (7 oz) strong white bread flour
½ teaspoon salt
½ teaspoon dried yeast
calorie controlled cooking spray
zero *ProPoints* value salad, to serve

For the topping
1 onion, chopped
400 g can chopped tomatoes
1 teaspoon dried oregano
100 g (3½ oz) chorizo, sliced thinly
1 red pepper, de-seeded and sliced thinly
50 g (1¾ oz) mozzarella light, sliced
100 g (3½ oz) half fat Cheddar cheese, grated
salt and freshly ground black pepper

9 *ProPoints* values per serving
37 *ProPoints* values per recipe

384 calories per serving

Takes **25 minutes** to prepare + **1–1½ hours** standing time, **8–10 minutes** to cook

✱ not recommended

1 Place the flour and salt in a large bowl. Make a well in the centre and add 125 ml (4 fl oz) of tepid water. Sprinkle over the yeast and leave to stand for 5 minutes.

2 Stir to dissolve the yeast and gradually draw in the flour to make a soft dough.

3 Turn out on to a floured surface and knead the dough until smooth. Place in a clean bowl that has been sprayed with the cooking spray, cover and leave to rise until doubled in size, about 1–1½ hours.

4 Meanwhile, to make the tomato sauce for the topping, heat a non stick frying pan and spray with the cooking spray. Cook the onion for 3–4 minutes until starting to soften, then add the tomatoes and oregano. Season well and cook for 8–10 minutes until slightly thickened. Remove from the heat.

5 Meanwhile, punch the dough to take out the air, shape into a ball and leave to rest in the bowl for a further 10 minutes.

6 Place the dough on a lightly floured surface and roll into a 30 cm (12 inch) round. Place on a baking tray. Preheat the oven to its hottest temperature and place a shelf near the top.

7 Spread the pizza with the tomato sauce and then lay the slices of chorizo and pepper on top. Finally, top with the slices of mozzarella cheese and grated Cheddar cheese. Bake in the oven for 8–10 minutes until the base is golden and the cheese is bubbling. Serve immediately, with the zero *ProPoints* value salad.

Variation If you prefer your pizzas really hot, sprinkle over a few slices of green chilli, for no additional *ProPoints* values.

Hungarian Goulash

A traditional Hungarian goulash – chunks of beef in a spicy, smooth sauce. Serve with a 225 g (8 oz) potato per person, baked in its skin, for an additional 5 **ProPoints** values.

Serves 1

calorie controlled cooking spray
175 g (6 oz) lean fillet steak, cubed
1 small onion, chopped
1 garlic clove, crushed
½ green pepper, de-seeded and sliced
2 teaspoons paprika
100 ml (3½ fl oz) beef stock
½ small can chopped tomatoes
2 teaspoons tomato purée
1 bouquet garni
50 g (1¾ oz) low fat fromage frais
salt and freshly ground black pepper

9 ProPoints values per serving
9 ProPoints values per recipe

C 422 calories per serving

Takes **25 minutes** to prepare,
20–25 minutes to cook

✱ recommended (for up to 1 month)

1 Preheat the oven to Gas Mark 4/180°C/fan oven 160°C. Heat a non stick pan, spray with the cooking spray and brown the steak for 4–5 minutes. Transfer to a small ovenproof dish.

2 Spray the pan with the cooking spray again, fry the onion until soft, then add the garlic and pepper and cook for another minute.

3 Stir in the paprika, cook for 1 minute and then add the stock, tomatoes, tomato purée and bouquet garni. Bring to the boil for a minute, season and pour over the beef.

4 Cook in the oven for 20–25 minutes until the beef is cooked. Remove the bouquet garni, stir in the fromage frais and serve immediately.

Prawn and Saffron Gumbo

Gumbo is a simple, thick and tasty stew from Louisiana. Serve with 60 g (2 oz) of dried white rice per person, cooked according to packet instructions, for an additional 6 **ProPoints** values per serving.

Serves 4

calorie controlled cooking spray
3 garlic cloves, crushed
3 shallots, chopped finely
2 carrots, peeled and diced
½ teaspoon dried chilli flakes
2 teaspoons coriander seeds
600 ml (20 fl oz) chicken or vegetable stock
400 g (14 oz) frozen prawns
250 g (9 oz) frozen sweetcorn
200 g (7 oz) cherry tomatoes, halved
200 g (7 oz) okra, green beans or mange tout, topped and sliced thinly
½ teaspoon Cajun spice mix (optional)
juice of ½ a lime
a small bunch of fresh parsley or coriander, chopped
salt and freshly ground black pepper

5 **ProPoints** value per serving
20 **ProPoints** values per recipe

C 239 **calories** per serving

Takes **35 minutes**

✱ not recommended

1 Heat a large non stick saucepan and spray with the cooking spray. Fry the garlic and shallots for 5 minutes or so, adding a little water if necessary to prevent them from sticking, until golden and softened.

2 Add the carrots, stir fry for a further 5 minutes and then add the chilli flakes, coriander seeds and stock and bring to the boil. Simmer for 5 minutes.

3 Add the prawns and sweetcorn, bring back to the boil and then simmer for 5 minutes. Add the tomatoes and okra, green beans or mange tout and simmer for a final 2 minutes, then add the Cajun spice mix, if using. Check the seasoning. Pour over the lime juice, scatter with the herbs and serve.

Tip To make your own Cajun spice mix, combine the following ingredients together in a food processor or pestle and mortar: 2 teaspoons each of salt, cayenne pepper and paprika, 2 bay leaves, 1 teaspoon each of black pepper, dried rosemary and dried chillies and ½ teaspoon each of white pepper, garlic powder, celery salt and ground allspice.

Moroccan Lamb

6 ProPoints value

If you fancy a change from burgers at your barbecue, try this delicious option.

Serves 4

For the lamb marinade

2 garlic cloves, crushed
1 teaspoon ground cumin
1 teaspoon coriander seeds, crushed
1 teaspoon paprika
½ teaspoon Cayenne pepper
1 small red chilli, de-seeded and chopped finely (optional)
2 tablespoons fresh coriander, chopped
2 tablespoons fresh flat leaf parsley, chopped
1 tablespoon olive oil
4 x 100 g (3½ oz) lean lamb leg steaks

For the salad

½ cucumber, peeled and diced
4 tomatoes, peeled, de-seeded and diced
½ red onion, diced
1 large red pepper, de-seeded and diced
1 teaspoon ground cumin
freshly ground rock salt
1 tablespoon fresh coriander, chopped, to garnish

---

6 ProPoints values per serving
26 ProPoints values per recipe

C **296 calories** per serving

Takes **15 minutes** to prepare + marinating, **10 minutes** to cook

✱ recommended

1 In a non metallic lidded bowl, thoroughly mix together all the marinade ingredients except the lamb. This will make a dry style marinade.

2 Score each lamb steak a few times without cutting right through the meat. Place the lamb in the marinade and turn over a few times to ensure it is thoroughly coated. Cover and put into the fridge for at least 3 hours, but preferably overnight.

3 To prepare the salad, place all of the salad vegetables in a serving dish and mix thoroughly. Just before serving, sprinkle the cumin over the salad, stir and season to taste. (If you do this earlier, the seasoning tends to make the vegetables a little soggy.) To garnish, sprinkle the chopped coriander over the top.

4 When you are ready to cook the meat, make sure the barbecue is hot, or preheat the grill to a medium-high heat. Grill the lamb steaks for 4–5 minutes on each side or until cooked to your liking, then serve with the salad.

Tip The longer you leave the marinade, the better the spices will be absorbed into the meat. In fact, this can be done 24 hours in advance.

Variation This recipe can be herby or have quite a kick. If you prefer the herby option, reduce the cayenne pepper to ¼ teaspoon and omit the chilli. The ProPoints values will remain the same.

Grilled Fish with a Spicy Moroccan Sauce

A fast and tasty dish. Serve with a zero **ProPoints** value green salad.

Serves 4

4 x 175 g (6 oz) cod steaks
salt and freshly ground black pepper

For the sauce

2 teaspoons cumin seeds
a small bunch of fresh coriander, chopped roughly
a small bunch of fresh mint, chopped
2 garlic cloves, chopped
1 red chilli, de-seeded and chopped
1 teaspoon paprika
a pinch of saffron
1–2 tablespoons low fat plain fromage frais
juice of a lemon

4 ProPoints values per serving
15 ProPoints values per recipe

168 calories per serving

Takes **5 minutes** to prepare,
15 minutes to cook

✱ not recommended

1 Toast the cumin seeds in a dry frying pan for 2 minutes, then set aside. Preheat the grill to high.

2 Place the fish steaks on the grill pan and season. Grill for 6–8 minutes on each side or until lightly browned and cooked through.

3 Mix all the sauce ingredients together in a bowl, including the cumin seeds. Season to taste with salt.

4 Spoon the sauce over the hot fish and serve.

Caribbean Chicken Pasta

For this sunshine-filled dish, spicy chicken fillets are paired with a cool refreshing salsa.

Serves 4

4 x 150 g (5½ oz) skinless boneless chicken breasts
350 g (12 oz) dried pasta

For the marinade

4 tablespoons reduced sugar lemon and lime marmalade
1 red chilli, de-seeded and chopped finely, or 1 teaspoon dried chilli flakes
2 tablespoons teriyaki sauce

For the salsa

250 g (9 oz) cherry tomatoes, halved
1 red onion, chopped finely
½ cucumber, chopped finely
1 green pepper, de-seeded and chopped finely
zest and juice of 2 limes
2 teaspoons sugar
salt and freshly ground black pepper

15 *ProPoints* values per serving
61 *ProPoints* values per recipe

618 calories per serving

Takes **10 minutes** to prepare, **20 minutes** to cook

✻ not recommended

1 Preheat the oven to Gas Mark 5/190°C/fan oven 170°C. Mix the marinade ingredients together in a small pan and heat, stirring, until combined.

2 Place the chicken breasts in an ovenproof dish and pour the marinade over. Cover with foil and bake in the oven for 10 minutes. Remove the foil, baste the chicken and cook, uncovered, for another 10 minutes, or until cooked through.

3 Meanwhile, bring a pan of water to the boil, add the pasta and cook according to packet instructions, then drain.

4 In a bowl, combine all the salsa ingredients.

5 Slice the chicken into thick pieces and toss the chicken into the warm pasta. Add the salsa and toss again. Check the seasoning and serve.

Spicy Lamb Chops with Fattoush

Fattoush is a Syrian and Lebanese salad of chopped salad vegetables with herbs and lemon and toasted flatbread. This makes a delicious, quick, midweek supper.

Serves 2

1 teaspoon cumin seeds, crushed

¼ teaspoon dried chilli flakes or small red chilli, de-seeded and chopped finely

zest and juice of a lemon

4 x 100 g (3½ oz) lamb chops on the bone, trimmed of visible fat

For the fattoush

2 pitta breads, torn into pieces

1 Little Gem lettuce, shredded

4 spring onions, sliced finely

½ cucumber, diced finely

1 green pepper, de-seeded and diced finely

2 ripe tomatoes, diced

grated zest and juice of a lemon

a few sprigs of fresh mint, chopped

a few sprigs of fresh coriander, chopped

a few sprigs of fresh parsley, chopped

salt and freshly ground black pepper

13 *ProPoints* values per serving
26 *ProPoints* values per recipe

595 calories per serving

Takes **20 minutes**

✱ not recommended

1 Preheat the oven to Gas Mark 7/220°C/fan oven 200°C. Place the cumin seeds, chilli and lemon zest and juice in a shallow bowl, add the lamb and rub in the mixture. Keep the lamb chops in the fridge while you make the salad.

2 To make the fattoush, spread out the pitta pieces on a baking tray. Toast in the oven for 10 minutes, or until crisp.

3 Meanwhile, combine all the other fattoush ingredients in a bowl. Preheat the grill to medium-high.

4 Grill the lamb chops for about 5–6 minutes on each side, until cooked as preferred. Toss the toasted pitta pieces into the salad and serve with the chops.

Kedgeree

A quick and easy version of the traditional smoked haddock and rice breakfast, lunch or supper dish.

Serves 4

175 g (6 oz) dried easy cook long-grain rice
a pinch of saffron threads (optional)
2 eggs
225 g (8 oz) smoked haddock fillets
calorie controlled cooking spray
1 onion, chopped
1 tablespoon curry powder
100 ml (3½ fl oz) chicken or vegetable stock
a bunch of fresh parsley, chopped
150 g (5½ oz) low fat natural yogurt

7 ProPoints values per serving
28 ProPoints values per recipe

C **272 calories** per serving

Takes **40 minutes**

✳ not recommended

1 Bring a pan of water to the boil, add the rice and saffron, if using, and cook for 10–15 minutes or according to packet instructions.

2 Meanwhile, bring another small pan of water to the boil, add the eggs and simmer for 8 minutes. Remove from the water and leave to cool.

3 Place the haddock in a shallow dish. Drain the rice, using the boiling water to pour over the haddock. Leave the haddock to stand for 5 minutes. Drain, remove the skin and any bones and then flake the fish coarsely.

4 Heat a non stick frying pan, spray with the cooking spray then fry the onion for 4 minutes until softened. Add the curry powder and cook a further 2 minutes. Peel the eggs and quarter them.

5 Stir the fish, onion, stock, eggs, parsley and yogurt into the cooked saffron rice, heat through and serve.

Variation Use a teaspoon of turmeric to achieve a yellow colour instead of the more expensive saffron.

Chermoula

This tomato based stew with broad beans originates in North Africa.

Serves 4

calorie controlled cooking spray
1 onion, sliced
200 g (7 oz) potatoes, peeled and diced
2 garlic cloves, crushed
1 teaspoon paprika
1 teaspoon ground cumin
a pinch of chilli flakes
150 ml (5 fl oz) vegetable stock
400 g can chopped tomatoes
175 g (6 oz) frozen broad beans
110 g (4 oz) frozen peas

To serve

1 tablespoon chopped fresh coriander
4 lemon wedges

1 Lightly spray a large, lidded, non stick saucepan with the cooking spray and heat until hot. Add the onion and cook, stirring, for 5 minutes. Add the potatoes and garlic and continue to cook for 2–3 minutes until they begin to brown. Add the spices and cook for a further minute.

2 Pour in the stock, tomatoes and broad beans. Bring to the boil and cover. Reduce the heat and cook for 20 minutes until the potatoes are tender. Stir in the peas and cook for a further 2 minutes until hot.

3 Serve the stew sprinkled with coriander and lemon wedges to squeeze over.

3 *ProPoints* values per serving
13 *ProPoints* values per recipe

C   146 calories per serving

Takes **15 minutes** to prepare, **25 minutes** to cook

V

✻   not recommended

Tip Sweet potato works well in this recipe too – replace 100 g (3½ oz) of potatoes with 100 g (3½ oz) of sweet potatoes. The *ProPoints* values will remain the same.

Caribbean Roast Pork

Serves 6

2 garlic cloves, crushed
1 teaspoon ground allspice
1 teaspoon ground mixed spice
1 teaspoon chilli flakes
juice of 2 limes
4 spring onions, chopped
1.5 kg (3 lb 5 oz) boneless pork shoulder, rind and fat removed

250 ml (9 fl oz) chicken stock
calorie controlled cooking spray
600 g (1 lb 5 oz) sweet potatoes, peeled and cut into chunks
300 g (10½ oz) parsnips, peeled and sliced
3 red onions, cut into chunks

1 Mix together the garlic, spices, lime juice and spring onions. Rub into the pork and put into a tight fitting dish. Cover with cling film and leave to marinate in the fridge for at least 12 hours.

2 Preheat the oven to Gas Mark 5/190°C/fan oven 170°C. Put the pork into a roasting tin and add 75 ml (3 fl oz) of the chicken stock. Cook for 1½–2 hours, basting regularly. After about 1¼ hours, spray another roasting tin with the cooking spray. Add the vegetables and roast for 1 hour, shaking and re-spraying a couple of times.

3 Remove the meat to a plate and leave it to rest for 20 minutes. Add the remaining chicken stock to the roasting tin and scrape up all the caramelised bits. Skim the fat off with a spoon and pour the juices only into a gravy boat. Serve three medium (35 g/1¼ oz) slices of pork per person with a helping of the vegetables and gravy.

11 ProPoints values per serving
68 ProPoints values per recipe

C 463 calories per serving

Takes **15 minutes** to prepare + marinating + resting, **2¼ hours** to cook

✳ recommended

Jamaican Chicken

This is a quick treat for those who like spicy food. Serve with a mixed zero **ProPoints** value salad and 60 g (2 oz) of dried white rice per person, cooked according to packet instructions, for an additional 6 **ProPoints** values per serving.

Serves 1

150 g (5½ oz) skinless boneless chicken breast
85 g (3 oz) jerk chicken marinade
salt and freshly ground black pepper

---

6 ProPoints values per serving
6 ProPoints values per recipe

C **250 calories** per serving

Takes **5 minutes** to prepare +
1 hour marinating, **15 minutes** to cook

✳ not recommended

1 Season the chicken, spread the marinade over it, cover and leave to marinate for 1 hour. Preheat the grill to medium.

2 Cook the chicken breast for 8 minutes on the first side. Turn and cook for 7 minutes on the second side. Serve at once.

Spicy Sausage Pasta

This is ultimate comfort food and takes just minutes to make.

Serves 4

350 g (12 oz) dried pasta
calorie controlled cooking spray
454 g packet low fat thick pork sausages, sliced
2 onions, sliced
2 garlic cloves, sliced
2 tablespoons dry white wine
6 sun-dried tomatoes
400 g can chopped tomatoes
1 red chilli, de-seeded and chopped finely, or
  1 teaspoon dried chilli flakes
¼ teaspoon ground nutmeg
½ teaspoon ground cloves
2 fresh sage sprigs, chopped, or 1 teaspoon
  dried sage, plus a little extra to garnish
300 ml (10 fl oz) stock
salt and freshly ground black pepper

17 ProPoints values per serving
69 ProPoints values per recipe

C **669 calories** per serving

Takes **5 minutes** to prepare,
25 minutes to cook

✳ recommended

1 Bring a pan of water to the boil, add the pasta and cook until al dente or according to packet instructions, then drain.

2 Meanwhile, heat a large non stick frying pan, spray with the cooking spray and brown the sausages all over. Add the onions and garlic and fry for 4 minutes or until softened.

3 Add the other ingredients to the frying pan and boil rapidly for 20 minutes or until the sauce is thick. Add the cooked pasta and toss together. Serve sprinkled with the extra fresh sage.

Tip If you can find them, use spicy low fat sausages.

Harissa Chicken with Papaya Raita ⓊⓄ 10 ProPoints value

A spicy Moroccan-style paste, known as harissa, makes this recipe especially delicious.

Serves 4

225 g (8 oz) dried bulgur wheat
3 spring onions, finely sliced
50 g (1¾ oz) ready to eat dried apricots, chopped
400 ml (14 fl oz) boiling water
1 tablespoon stir fry oil or vegetable oil
450 g (1 lb) skinless boneless chicken breasts, diced
1–2 tablespoons harissa paste or 3 teaspoons chilli sauce
1 red pepper, de-seeded and chopped
1 yellow pepper, de-seeded and chopped
1 large courgette, chopped
salt

For the raita
1 papaya, finely chopped (see Tip)
5 tablespoons low fat natural yogurt
1 tablespoon chopped fresh mint

⒞ **10 ProPoints** values per serving
39 ProPoints values per recipe

C **424 calories** per serving

⊙ Takes **20 minutes** to prepare,
15 minutes to cook

✳ not recommended

1 Put the bulgur wheat into a heatproof bowl with a generous pinch of salt, the spring onions and apricots. Cover with the boiling water and leave to soak for 10 minutes.

2 Meanwhile, heat the oil in a non stick wok or frying pan and add the chicken, cooking and stirring it for 4–5 minutes, until browned. Add the harissa paste (1 tablespoon if you prefer a milder flavour, 2 tablespoons if you like your food spicy) and cook over a medium heat, stirring, for another 2–3 minutes.

3 Add the peppers and courgette and cook for another 5–6 minutes, stirring often, until the vegetables are cooked, but not mushy.

4 Meanwhile, make the raita by mixing together the papaya, yogurt and mint. Cover and chill until ready to serve.

5 Reheat the bulgur wheat, either by microwaving it for about 1 minute on High or by steaming it over a pan of simmering water. Fluff up with a fork, then divide between four serving plates. Top with the chicken mixture and serve with the raita.

Tips To prepare a papaya, slice it in half, scoop out the inedible black seeds, then peel.

Harissa paste is a Moroccan blend of garlic, chillies, caraway and salt and is now readily available in major supermarkets.

Variations Not keen on papaya? Then use a 10 cm (4 inch) piece of cucumber, finely chopped, for the raita. The **ProPoints** values will remain the same.

You could also replace the bulgur wheat with the same amount of dried couscous, for a **ProPoints** value of 11 per serving.

Index